Hymns & Carols

Hymns & Carols

Edited by Tony Jasper

CRESSET

To Jack Heather, Sidney Thomas, John North, Fred Semmons, Harold H. Harvey, Sydney Quick, Jack Matthews and Douglas Matthews. They encouraged my preaching and taught me the joy of singing hymns and carols.

First published in Great Britain in 1983 by Frederick Muller Limited, Dataday House, London SW19 7JZ

Copyright © 1983 by Tony Jasper

This edition published in 1992 by Cresset

ISBN 0 09 177205 2

Printed and bound by Thomson Press, India.

Contents

Preface

Here is a collection of some of the best loved Christmas, Easter and Harvest hymns and carols. The accent is unashamedly on the word 'popular' but one or two selections should at the very least surprise and, hopefully, delight.

The material is intended to be sung. The many pictures and the text should aid understanding and provide a base for prayer and reflection. Content extends the Christian denominational boundaries and certainly the material comes from many Christian traditions and countries.

I have dug back into popular hymnody and resurrected some old favourites which have — for one reason or another — been omitted from post-war denominational collections. *The Gospel Bells Are Ringing* is included as the popular harvest song which is best known under the title of *Bringing In The Sheaves*, while in the harvest-of-the-sea section there is space for *Throw Out The Life-Line* and *Jesus Saviour, Pilot Me*. Lovers of the wonderful hymns of the Wesleys will be doubtless surprised and I think delighted with the inclusion of *Join, All Ye Joyful Nations*, which for some inexplicable reason was left out of the Methodist Hymn Books of 1904 and 1932.

Several American favourites like *Joy To The World* (although the lyricist is Isaac Watts) and *O Holy Night* are included. There is a place for comparatively new carols such as the captivating *Il Est Né* and *Jesus, Jesus, Rest Your Head*. I have taken the licence of including my personal favourite, the little known carol *Remember O Thou Man*, as well as a tune I grew up with in Cornwall, Merritt's sturdy composition for *Hark The Glad Sound*. Again, it is a pleasure to be able to include some splendid British carols which, due to their exclusion from most major British denominational hymnbooks, receive little attention when compared with say *Once In Royal David's City* or *Hark! The Herald Angels Sing*. Thus you will find in this volume *I Saw Three Ships*, *We Three Kings Of Orient Are*, the *Coventry Carol*, *The Holly Bears A Berry*, *Down in Yon Forest* and others. Several selections have a folkish air as for instance *Born In The Night (Mary's Child)* and *Every Star Shall Sing A Carol*, while from the pop charts there comes the Steeleye Span version of *Gaudete*, which was a hit in 1973. There is included Bob Dylan's memorable *Father Of Night* from his album New Morning.

As any hymn-book compiler knows full well, it is no easy task to choose the 'right' tune. In some cases there is no dispute, in others confusion reigns. The best example must be *O Little Town Of Bethlehem*, though I confess I enjoy each and every one of the many tunes associated with this hymn. Space forbids the inclusion of every alternative accompaniment to particular hymns, but where it has been possible several tunes are given, especially when two great hymn-singing countries like America and Britain clash and where the exclusion of one would leave the other nation in a state of bewilderment!

The compilation of a volume such as this is far from an easy task and the juggling of words, tunes, prefaces, pictures etcetera is a nightmare, more so because this volume comprises several sections under each of the main topics mentioned so that under Christmas there is Advent, Birth, Epiphany and a logical progression of material under General Celebration, Announcement of Birth, the Virgin Mary, Birth, Shepherds and Wise Men, although there is some overlapping. I have included hymns and carols which link Christmas and Easter, and the Easter songs which tell of Good Friday and Easter Sunday; next comes harvest of the land and of the sea. Finally a word of thanks must go to various people with whom I have talked and discussed the book's eventual shape: to Rosalie Vickers-Harris, Vicky Sinha, John J. Matthews, John Phillpots, Joyce Horn, Margaret Palmer, Clive Thexton, Janet A. Baxendale and especially my music copy writer and arranger when needed, Brian Coleman. Not least thanks to Moira O'Donnell, Editor at Mullers, and others at the publishing house and to the talented artists whose commissioned work adorns some of these pages. Their names are given in the end credits.

Good reading, reflection and above all 'praise'.

Tony Jasper

Joy To The World

Psalm 98 provided the inspiration for this carol by Isaac Watts.
His sentiments catch the flavour of Luke 2:10 — 'I bring you
good news of a great joy which will come *to all people.*'

Antioch   *G.F. Handel, 1742*

Joy to the world! the Lord is come: Let earth re-ceive her King. Let ev-'ry heart pre-pare Him room, And heaven and na-ture sing, And heaven and na-ture sing, And hea-v'n, and heav'n and na-ture sing.

2. Joy to the world! the Saviour reigns!
   Let men their songs employ;
   While fields and floods, rocks, hills and plains
   Repeat the sounding joy (repeat three times).

3. He rules the world with truth and grace,
   And makes the nations prove
   The glories of his righteousness
   And wonders of his love (repeat three times).

   from Psalm 98. Isaac Watts

Ding Dong Merrily On High

Earth and heaven tell the same joyful story and the sound
whether of bells or voices is deafening — Glory to God in the
Highest (Luke 2:14) — the Saviour comes. The tune is a

Words by G.R. Woodward

*16th century French tune
harmonised by Charles Wood*

Ding dong! mer - ri - ly on high, in heav'n the bells are ring - ing:

Ding dong! ve - ri - ly the sky is riv'n with an - gels sing - ing.

Glo - - - - - - - - - - ri - a, Ho - san - na in ex - cel - sis!

2. E'en so here below, below,
   Let steeple bells be swungen,
   And i-o, i-o, i-o,
   By priest and people sungen.
   Gloria, Hosanna in excelsis!

3. Pray you, dutifully prime
   Your matin chime, ye ringers;
   May you beautifully rime
   Your evetime song, ye singers;
   Gloria, hosanna in excelsis!

   G.R. Woodward

Good Christian Men Rejoice

A French dialect carol, possibly 14th century. Neal's version
appeared in 1853. The joyful tidings are proclaimed and people
invited to experience their significance. Jesus is properly called
'the' Saviour — He 'saves' the world and he can do this because
he was the Son of God. The writer says 'he was born for this'.

In dulci jubilo

Weihnachtslied, 14th century

Good Christ - ian men re - joice _____ With heart and soul and voice! _____

Give ye heed to what we say: News! News! Je - sus Christ is born to - day.

Ox and ass be - fore him bow, And He is in the man - ger now:

Christ is born to - day. _____ Christ is born to - day. _____

2. Good Christian men, rejoice
   With heart and soul and voice!
     Now ye hear of endless bliss:
       Joy! Joy!
     Jesus Christ was born for this.
   He hath oped the heavenly door,
   And man is blest for evermore.
     Christ was born for this.

3. Good Christian men, rejoice
   With heart and soul and voice!
     Now ye need not fear the grave:
       Peace! Peace!
     Jesus Christ was born to save;
   Calls you one, and calls you all,
   To gain His everlasting hall.
     Christ was born to save.

John Mason Neale, 1818-66

Gaudete

The words were written in 1582 but this arrangement is by the
members of Steeleye Span. The group's recording made the
British pop charts in 1973.

*Arranged by Timothy Hart, Peter Knight,
Frederick Kemp, Madelaine Prior and Robert Johnson*

Traditional

♩ = 192

REFRAIN

Gau - de - te, Gau - de - te, Chris - tus est na - tus

Ex Ma - ri - a vir - gin - ae, Gau - de - te.

1. Tem - pus ad - est gra - ti - ae   Hoc quod op - ta - ba - mus,
2. De - us ho - mo fac - tus est,   Na - tu - ra mi - ran - te,
3. Ez - e - che - e - lis por - ta   Clau - sa per - trans - i - tur,
4. Er - go nos - tra con - ti - o   Psal - lat jam in lus - tro,

Repeat Refrain

Car - min - a lae - ti - ti - ae   De - vo - te red - da - mus.
Mun - dus re - no - va - tus est   A Chris - to re - gnan - te.
Un - de lux est or - ta   Sa - lus in - ve - ni - tur.
Ben - e - di - cat do - mi - no,   Sa - lus Re - gi nos - tro.

17

Every Star Shall Sing A Carol

Hymns And Songs — the supplement to the Methodist Church hymn-book — sub-title this 'A Carol of the Universe'. Carter is a poet and songwriter, arguably one of the few adventurous creative writers of contemporary religious verse.

Sydney Carter (1915-)

The Waits

We come a-singing to your gates,
So listen at your leisure!
We are the merry Christmas waits,
Who wish you peace & pleasure!

A Very Happy Christmas

2. When the King of all creation
      Had a cradle on the earth,
   Holy was the human body,
      Holy was the human birth:

3. Who can tell what other cradle,
      High above the Milky Way,
   Still may rock the King of Heaven
      On another Christmas Day?

4. Who can count how many crosses,
      Still to come or long ago,
   Crucify the King of Heaven?
      Holy is the name I know.

5. Who can tell what other body
      He will hallow for his own?
   I will praise the son of Mary,
      Brother of my blood and bone.

6. Every star and every planet,
      Every creature, high and low,
   Come and praise the King of Heaven
      By whatever name you know.

Sydney Carter (1915-

Love came down at Christmas,
Love all lovely, love divine;
Love was born at Christmas,
Star and angels gave the sign.

Love shall be our token,
Love be yours and love be mine,
Love to God and all men,
Love for plea and gift and sign.

Christina Georgina Rossetti

My heart for very joy doth leap,
My lips no more their silence keep;
I too must sing with joyful tongue
That sweetest ancient cradle-song.

Martin Luther

And to those who have never listened
To the message of thy birth,
Who have winter, but no Christmas
Bringing them thy peace on earth,
Send to these the joyful tidings;
By all people, in each home,
Be there heard the Christmas anthem:
Praise to God, the Christ has come!

George Stringer Rowe

Stupendous height of heavenly love,
Of pitying tenderness divine;
It brought the Saviour from above,
It caused the springing day to shine;
The sun of righteousness to appear,
And gild our gloomy hemisphere.

Charles Wesley

Some say that ever 'gainst that season comes
Wherein our Saviour's birth is celebrated,
The bird of dawning singeth all night long:
And then, they say, no spirit dare walk abroad;
The nights are wholesome; then no planets strike,
No fairy takes, nor witch has power to charm,
So hallow'd and so gracious is the time.

William Shakespeare, Hamlet, *1.1.*

It came upon the midnight clear,
That glorious song of old,
From angels bending near the earth
To touch their harps of gold:
Peace on earth, good-will to men,
From heaven's all-gracious King!
The world in solemn stillness lay
To hear the angels sing.

Edward Hamilton Sears

Deck The Halls With Boughs Of Holly

Secular and religious sentiments merge in this traditional carol.
In the Oxford Book of Carols the Welsh tune is set to
accompany Now The Joyful Bells A-Ringing.

Nos Galan

Traditional Welsh

Deck the hall with boughs of hol - ly, Fa la la la la la la la la,

'Tis the sea - son to be jol - ly, Fa la la la la la la la la.

Fill the mead cup, drain the bar - rel, Fa la la la la la la la la,

Troll the an - cient Christ - mas car - ol, Fa la la la la la la la la.

2. See the flowing bowl before us,
   Fa la la la la la la, la, la.
   Strike the harp and join the chorus,
   Fa la. &c.
   Follow me in merry measure,
   Fa la. &c.
   While I sing of beauty's treasure,
   Fa la. &c.

3. Fast away the old year passes,
   Fa la la la la la la, la, la.
   Hail the new, ye lads and lassies,
   Fa la. &c.
   Laughing, quaffing, all together,
   Fa la. &c.
   Heedless of the wind and weather.
   Fa la. &c.

Traditional

We Wish You A Merry Christmas

The title is 'the' Christmas greeting and the tune is British,
West Country in origin. The pudding — the climax of the British
Christmas Day meal — was at one time a fasting dish but is now
an immensely rich concoction and decidedly heavy on the
stomach.

Traditional West Country. Arranged by Brian Coleman

We wish you a merry Christmas, We wish you a merry Christmas, We wish you a merry Christmas, And a happy New Year.

Good tidings we bring To you and your kin, We wish you a merry Christmas, And a happy New Year.

2. Now bring us some figgy pudding,
   Now bring us some figgy pudding,
   Now bring us some figgy pudding,
   And bring some out here.

   Good tidings we bring
   To you and your kin,
   We wish you a merry Christmas
   And a happy New Year.

3. For we all like figgy pudding
   We all like figgy pudding,
   For we all like figgy pudding,
   So bring some out here.

4. And we won't go till we've got some,
   We won't go, till we've got some,
   And we won't go till we've got some,
   So bring some out here.

Traditional

25

O Come, Immanuel

The derivation is the 12th Century Antiphons in Latin Breviary. The Antiphon was a short sentence. In this instance a long-drawn out "O!" sufficed in the early church rubric — expressive of a deep yearning for Christ's return — spoken before or after the Magnificat. Later Scriptural titles for Jesus became added and on each of the seven days leading to Christmas one was chanted. Eventually a Latin hymn came from these ascriptions.

Hymnal Noted, 1854

In free rhythm

O come, O come, Im-man - u - el, And ran-som cap-tive Is - ra - el,

That mourns in lone-ly ex - ile here Un-til the Son of God ___ ap-pear.

Re-joice! Re-joice! Im - man - u - el shall come to thee, O Is - ra - el.

2. O come, O come, Thou Lord of might,
   Who to Thy tribes, on Sinai's height,
   In ancient times didst give the law
   In cloud, and majesty, and awe.

3. O come, Thou Rod of Jesse, free
   Thine own from Satan's tyranny;
   From depths of hell Thy people save.
   And give them victory o'er the grave.

4. O come, Thou Day-spring, come and cheer
   Our spirits by Thine advent here;
   Disperse the gloomy clouds of night,
   And death's dark shadows put to flight.

5. O come, Thou Key of David, come,
   And open wide our heavenly home;
   Make safe the way that leads on high,
   And close the path to misery.

From Antiphons in Latin Breviary, 12th century
tr. by John Mason Neale, 1818-66

Hark The Glad Sound!

Doddridge wrote his popular Advent hymn on December 28, 1735 with Luke, chapter four, verses 18 and 19 very much in mind. The good news is for those who have need. The Jesus who came, comes and will come again.

[FIRST TUNE]

Bristol   *Ravenscroft's psalter, 1621*

Hark the glad sound! the Saviour comes, The Saviour promised long: Let

ev-'ry heart pre-pare a throne, And ev-'ry voice a song.

2. He comes the prisoners to release,
   In Satan's bondage held;
   The gates of brass before Him burst,
   The iron fetters yield.

3. He comes the broken heart to bind,
   The bleeding soul to cure,
   And with the treasures of His grace
   To enrich the humble poor.

4. Our glad hosannas, Prince of Peace,
   Thy welcome shall proclaim
   And heaven's eternal arches ring
   With Thy beloved name.

Philip Doddridge, 1702-51

Hark the Glad Sound!   Thomas Merritt

Hark the glad sound! — the Sa - viour comes, The Sa - viour pro - mised

long, The Sa - viour pro - mised long; Let ev - 'ry

heart pre - pare — a throne, Let ev - 'ry heart — pre -

And ev - 'ry voice a song, And ev - 'ry voice a

pare a — throne, And ev - 'ry voice — a — song,
                                                            And ev - 'ry voice a
                                                                              And

song.
              And ev - 'ry voice a song.
song,
ev - 'ry voice — a song, And ev - 'ry voice a — song.

29

Come Thou Long-Expected Jesus

Originally Wesley wrote two verses of eight lines. The lyric flies
in the face of those who would see Jesus as someone who
expounded a noble way of living but no more. Wesley captures
New Testament teaching which sees Jesus as someone who frees
men and women from all forces — physical, intellectual or
spiritual — which stultify their lives.

Stuttgart

C.F. Witt, c. 1660-1716

Come, thou long ex-pec-ted Je-sus, Born to set Thy peo-ple free,

From our fears and sins re-lease us, Let us find our rest in Thee.

2. Israel's strength and consolation,
    Hope of all the earth Thou art;
  Dear Desire of every nation,
    Joy of every longing heart.

3. Born Thy people to deliver,
    Born a child and yet a king,
  Born to reign in us for ever,
    Now Thy gracious kingdom bring.

4. By Thine own eternal Spirit
    Rule in all our hearts alone;
  By Thine all-sufficient merit
    Raise us to Thy glorious throne.
                    Amen.

Charles Wesley, 1707-88

Christmas won't be Christmas
Without any presents.

Louisa May Alcott
Little Women

Christmas is coming,
    The geese are getting fat,
Please to put a penny
    In the old man's hat;
If you haven't got a penny,
    A ha'penny will do.
If you haven't got a ha'penny,
God bless you!

Anonymous

And I without tarrying
Went into the caroling.

Chaucer

Rejoice if you are good,
For you are drawing nearer to your goal!
Rejoice, if you are less than good,
For your Saviour offers you pardon!
And if you are a non-believer rejoice,
For God calls you to life!

Pope St. Leo. Christmas Homily

Let us learn of those sages,
Who were wise, to obey.
Nay, we find through all ages
They have honoured this day,
Ever since our Redeemer's
Blest nativity,
Who was born of a virgin
To set sinners free.

This New Christmas Carol. Traditional

Therefore, Christian men, be sure,
Wealth or rank possessing,
Ye who now will bless the poor,
Shall yourselves find blessing.

Good King Wenceslas

Now that the time is come wherein
Our Saviour Christ was born,
The larders full of beef and pork,
And garners filled with corn;

With mutton, veal, beef, pig and pork,
Well furnish every board —
Plum-pudding, furmity, and what
Thy stock will then afford.

an old English Christmas Carol

Of Christmas
We can never tire
Time of friendly cheer
Place the Yule
Log on the fire
To warm old
Christmas
Here.

from an old English Christmas card

The dinner itself was a prodigious feast.
The cookstove must have rested and panted
For a week thereafter.

from Chimney-Pot-Papers,
Charles S. Brooks.

Join All Ye Joyful Nations

A Wesley composition which is strangely neglected, even by
Methodists. The news is joyful, telling of a birthday where a gift
of life is given. The event in its operation and meaning contrasts
with conventional worldly values, sentiments and systems which
rest on money, might and force rather than true caring, respect
and the giving of love.

Lostwithiel

J. Turle, 1853

Join, all ye joy-ful nat-ions. The ac-claim-ing host of heav-en!
This hap-py morn A Child is born, To us a Son is
giv-en: The mes-seng-er and tok-en of God's et-er-nal fav-our, God
hath sent down To us His Son, A un-iv-er-sal Sa-viour.

2. The wonderful Messiah,
   The Joy of every nation,
     Jesus his name,
     With God the same,
   The Lord of all creation:
   The Counsellor of sinners,
   Almighty to deliver,
     The Prince of Peace
     Whose love's increase
   Shall reign in man for ever.

3. Go see the King of Glory,
   Discern the heavenly stranger,
     So poor and mean,
     His court an inn,
   His cradle is a manger:
   Who from His Father's bosom
   But now for us descended,
     Who built the skies,
     On earth he lies
   With only beasts attended.

4. Whom all the angels worship
   Lies hid in human nature;
     Incarnate see
     The Deity,
   The infinite Creator:
   See the stupendous blessing
   Which God to us hath given,
     A child of man,
     In length a span,
   Who fills both earth and heaven.

5. Gaze on that helpless Object
   Of endless adoration!
     Those infant hands
     Shall burst our bands,
   And work out our salvation:
   Strangle the crooked serpent,
   Destroy his works for ever,
     And open set
     The heavenly gate
   To every true believer.

6. Till then, Thou holy Jesus,
   We humbly bow before Thee,
     Our treasures bring
     To serve our King,
   And joyfully adore Thee:
   To Thee we gladly render
   Whate'er Thy grace hath given,
     Till Thou appear
     In glory here,
   And take us up to heaven.

Charles Wesley

The Virgin Mary Had A Baby Boy

'They say his name was Jesus' – 'Jesus', in the Grecianised form of the Hebrew name, means 'God Saves' for Jesus brings God and man together. This catchy, rhythmic carol has become increasingly popular with young people during the last five years.

From the Edric Connor Collection;
arr. T.B.C.

The Vir-gin Ma-ry had a ba-by boy, — The Vir-gin Ma-ry had a ba-by boy, — The

Vir-gin Ma-ry had a ba-by boy, And they say that his name was Je-sus. — He come from the

CHORUS

glo - ry — He come from the glo-rious King-dom; He come from the glo - ry —

He come from the glo-rious King-dom; Oh yes! be-liev-er, Oh

yes! be-liev-er,   He come from the glo - ry —   He come from the glo-rious King-dom.

2 The angels sang when the babe was born,
  The angels sang when the babe was born,
  The angels sang when the babe was born,
  And proclaimed him the Saviour Jesus.
    Chorus

3 The wise men saw where the babe was born,
  The wise men saw where the babe was born,
  The wise men saw where the babe was born,
  And they saw that his name was Jesus.
    Chorus

From the Edric Connor Collection

Now The Holly Bears A Berry

Also known as the *Sans Day Carol,* this song comes from St. Day
in the parish of Gwennap, Cornwall and was collected orally by
a Mr. W.D. Watson who sang it to the Rev. G.H. Doble after
hearing it sung by an old man, Mr. Thomas Beard, at St. Day.
The Cornish version is Ma Gron War'n Gelinen.

Cornish   *Arr. Martin Shaw*

Now the hol - ly bears a ber - ry as white as the milk, And —

Ma - ry bore — Je - sus, who was wrapped up in silk: And — Ma - ry bore —

Je - sus Christ our Sa - viour for to be, And the first tree in the green-wood, it was the hol -

ly, hol - ly, hol - ly! And the first tree in the green-wood, it was the hol - ly!

2. Now the holly bears a berry as green as the grass,
   And Mary bore Jesus, who died on the cross:

3. Now the holly bears a berry as black as the coal,
   And Mary bore Jesus, who died for us all:

4. Now the holly bears a berry, as blood is it red,
   Then trust we our Saviour, who rose from the dead:

Arr. Martin Shaw

Down In Yon Forest

A strange yet rather beautiful 15th century folk carol which has undergone various textual changes over the years. The melody and text (save *flood* for *river* and *bed's foot* for *foot of the bed*) were taken from Mr. Hall, Castleton, Derbyshire by Ralph Vaughan Williams. The marvellous *Oxford Book Of Carols* gives a similar *All Bells In Paradise* which, like *Down In Yon Forest*, has a eucharistic flavour.

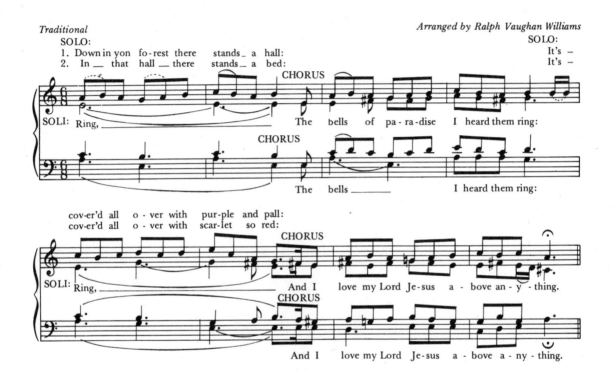

Traditional

Arranged by Ralph Vaughan Williams

SOLO:
1. Down in yon fo-rest there stands a hall:
2. In that hall there stands a bed:

SOLO:
It's —

SOLI: Ring, The bells of pa-ra-dise I heard them ring:

CHORUS
The bells I heard them ring:

cov-er'd all o-ver with pur-ple and pall:
cov-er'd all o-ver with scar-let so red:

SOLI: Ring, And I love my Lord Je-sus a-bove an-y-thing.

CHORUS
And I love my Lord Je-sus a-bove a-ny-thing.

3. At the bedside there lies a stone;
   Which the sweet Virgin Mary knelt upon:

4. Under that bed there runs a flood:
   The one half runs water, the other runs blood:

5. At the bed's foot there grows a thorn:
   Which ever blows blossom since he was born:

6. Over that bed the moon shines bright:
   Denoting our Saviour was born this night:

Arr. Ralph Vaughan Williams

Note. It is suggested that the solo portion be sung without harmony in the opening verses, also that the solo portion be divided among various voices (male and female).

The Holly And The Ivy

Another mixture of the secular and the religious, this carol is in
all likelihood pagan in origin. As the *Oxford Book of Carols*
notes, it symbolizes the masculine (holly) and feminine (ivy)
elements, as 'the tribal chorus developed into dialogue, all such
songs being sung as a dance between the lads and the maids.'
The lack of success experienced by the early Church, in banning
the use of pagan evergreen customs from religious circles, led to
her 'christianizing' these popular seasonal traditions.

This carol may be sung with or without accompaniment.

play - ing of —— the —— mer - ry or - gan Sweet sing -ing in the choir.

2. The holly bears a blossom,
   As white as the lily flower,
   And Mary bore sweet Jesus Christ,
   To be our sweet Saviour:

3. The holly bears a berry,
   As red as any blood,
   And Mary bore sweet Jesus Christ,
   To do poor sinners good:

4. The holly bears a prickle,
   As sharp as any thorn,
   And Mary bore sweet Jesus Christ,
   On Christmas Day in the morn:

5. The holly bears a bark,
   As bitter as any gall,
   And Mary bore sweet Jesus Christ,
   For to redeem us all:

Joseph Dearest Joseph Mine

Originally intended to be sung as part of a Mystery Play this
15th century German composition is to be found in a
manuscript at Leipzig University. It is easily adapted for a short
Christmas play with verses 1 and 2 sung by Joseph and Mary and
the chorus by children. The remaining verses can be sung by one
or more men and women.

Tr. N.S.T.   *Arr. Ralph Vaughan Williams*

par - a - dise, So prays the mo - ther Ma - ry.
par - a - dise, As prays the mo - ther Ma - ry.
lies so still With - in the crib of Ma - ry.
all may see In Je - sus, Son of Ma - ry.

CHORUS

He came a-mong us at Christ-mas-tide, At Christ-mas-tide, In Beth-le-hem;

Men shall bring him from far and wide Love's di - a - dem: Je - sus,

Je - sus, Lo, he comes, and loves, and saves, and frees us!

5. Now is born Em - man - u - el, Pro - phe- sied once by E -
6. Thou my la - zy heart has stirred, Thou, the Fa - ther's e -
7. Sweet and love - ly lit - tle one, Thou prince - ly, beau - ti - ful,
8. Lit - tle man, and God in - deed, Lit - tle and poor, thou art

ze - ki - el, Pro - mis'd Ma - ry by Ga - bri - el Ah,
ter - nal Word, Great - er than aught___ that ear hath heard, Thou
God's own Son, With - out thee all of us were un - done; Our
all we need; We will fol - low where thou dost lead, And

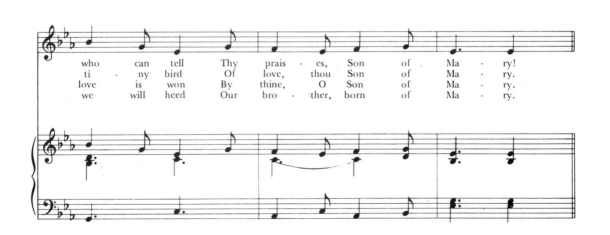

who can tell Thy prais - es, Son of Ma - ry!
ti - ny bird Of love, thou Son of Ma - ry.
love is won By thine, O Son of Ma - ry.
we will heed Our bro - ther, born of Ma - ry.

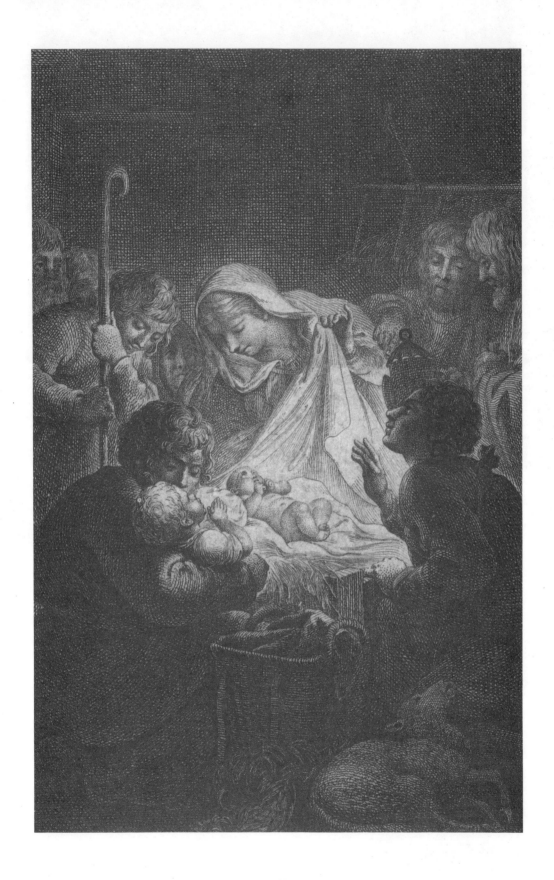

I Saw Three Ships Come Sailing By

The carol is found in all early British broadsheets and shared
early popularity with *God Rest You Merry Gentlemen* and *The
Seven Joys*. The version given here is from Sandys, 1833.
Another tune is found in the *English Carol Book* (P. Dearmer
and M. Shaw, Mowbray).

Traditional   *Ibid. (M.S.)*

4. Pray, whither sailed those ships all three?

5. O, they sailed into Bethlehem.

6. And all the bells on earth shall ring.

7. And all the angels in heaven shall sing.

8. And all the souls on earth shall sing.

9. Then let us all rejoice again!

The First Nowell

It is strange that, for all its popularity, there should be nothing known about the author or source of this carol. Some chroniclers suggest it comes from the 17th century, while others hold that the version given here dates from the early 19th century. Magi is from *magikos*, magician, magic, and these 'wise men' probably belonged with 'a stream of wisdom seekers in the Ancient Near East'. (*Black's Bible Dictionary*).

Sandys Collection, 1833

The first Now-ell the an-gel did say was to cer-tain poor shep-herds in fields as they lay: In fields where they lay a-keep-ing their sheep On a cold win-ter's night that was so deep. Now-ell, Now-ell Now-ell, Now-ell, Born is the King of Is-ra-el.

2. They looked up and saw a star,
   Shining in the east, beyond them far,
   And to the earth it gave great light,
   And so it continued both day and night.

3. And by the light of that same star,
   Three wise men came from country far;
   To seek for a King was their intent,
   And to follow the star wherever it went.

4. This star drew nigh to the north-west,
   O'er Bethlehem it took its rest,
   And there it did both stop and stay
   Right over the place where Jesus lay.

5. Then entered in those wise men three,
   Full reverently upon their knee,
   And offered there in His presence
   Their gold and myrrh and frankincense.

6. Then let us all with one accord
   Sing praises to our Heavenly Lord,
   That hath made heaven and earth of nought,
   And with His blood mankind hath bought.

Anonymous

Unto Us A Child Is Born

The original melody and words of *Puer Nobis Nascitur* can be found in a Trier manuscript of the 15th century. Many variants have existed. This beautiful carol has become increasingly popular in British circles and has been finding its way into some modern denominational hymn-book selections.

Unison

Piae Cantiones, 1581 Geoffrey Shaw

Un - to us a boy is born! King of all cre - a - tion, Came he to a world for - lorn, The Lord of ev -'ry na - - - tion.

2. Cradled in a stall was he
   With sleepy cows and asses;
   But the very beasts could see
   That he all men surpasses.

3. Herod then with fear was filled:
   'A prince', he said, 'in Jewry!'
   All the little boys he killed
   At Bethlehem in his fury.

4. Now Mary's son, who came
   So long ago to love us,
   Lead us all with hearts aflame
   Unto the joys above us.

5. Omega and Alpha be!
   Let the organ thunder,
   While the choir with peals of glee
   Doth rend the air as under.

15th century. Translated O.B.C.

Christians Awake Salute The Happy Sound

Writer John Byrom was a friend of John and Charles Wesley.
His hymn is compiled from a poem of 48 lines given in his
Poems of 1773. Byrom promised his favourite daughter, Dolly,
that he would write her something special as a Christmas
present; on the Christmas morning of 1745 she found an
envelope inscribed 'Christmas Day for Dolly', which contained
this hymn. His hymn is perfect for the 'Days of days'.

Yorkshire

J. Wainwright, 1723-68

Christ - ians, a - wake, sal - ute the hap - py morn, Where - on the Sa - viour of man -

kind was born; Rise to ad - ore the mys - te - ry of love,

Which hosts of an - gels chant - ed from a - bove; With them the joy - ful

tid - ings first be gun Of God in - car - nate and the Vir - gin's Son.

2. Then to the watchful shepherds it was told,
   Who heard the angelic herald's voice: Behold,
   I bring good tidings of a Saviour's birth
   To you and all the nations upon earth;
   This day hath God fulfilled His promised word,
   This day is born a Saviour, Christ the Lord.

3. He spake; and straightway the celestial choir
   In hymns of joy, unknown before, conspire.
   The praises of redeeming love they sang,
   And heaven's whole orb with hallelujahs rang;
   God's highest glory was their anthem still,
   Peace upon earth, and unto men good-will.

4. To Bethlehem straight the enlightened shepherds ran,
   To see the wonder God had wrought for man:
   Then to their flocks, still praising God, return,
   And their glad hearts with holy rapture burn;
   Amazed, the wondrous tidings they proclaim,
   The first apostles of His infant fame.

J. Wainwright, 1723-68

O Come All Ye Faithful

17th or 18th century in date; authorship of French or German
derivation, probably a Latin hymn. Adeste Fideles, Laeti
Triumphantes, has eight verses in some early sources. Frederick
Oakley translated the Latin text in 1841 for use at Margaret
Street Chapel, London, where he was then incumbent. The tune
dates to a 1751 manuscript, published in 1782 and harmonized
by Vincent Novello in 1797 and sung at the Chapel of the
Portuguese Embassy, where he was organist. He names John
Reading, organist of Winchester Cathedral as the composer.

Adeste Fideles

J.F. Wade's MS Book. 1751

2. True God of true God,
   Light of light eternal,
   Lo, he abhors not the virgin's womb,
   Son of the Father,
   Begotten, not created:

3. Sing, choirs of angels,
   Sing in exultation,
   Sing, all ye citizens of heaven above:
   Glory to God
   In the highest:

4. Yea, Lord, we greet thee,
   Born this happy morning;
   Jesu, to thee be glory given,
   Word of the Father,
   Now in flesh appearing:

   Anon, tr. Frederick Oakley, 1802-80

(The refrain is sung after each verse)

O Holy Night

Holy Night

Adolphe Adam, 1803-56

O ho-ly night! the stars are bright-ly shin-ing, It is the night of the dear Sa-viour's

birth; Long lay the world in sin and er-ror pin-ing, Till he ap-peared and the soul felt its

worth. A thrill of hope the wea-ry soul re-joi-ces, For yon-der breaks a new and glo-rious morn;

Fall on your knees, Oh, hear the an-gel voi-ces! O night di-

vine _____ O night _____ when Christ was born! O night _____ O ho - ly

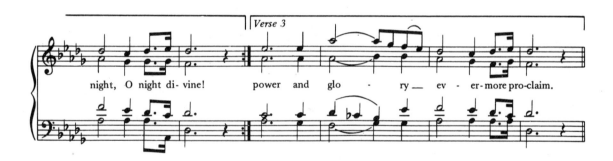

night, O night di- vine! power and glo - ry _ ev - er-more pro-claim.

2. Led by the light of faith serenely beaming,
   With glowing hearts by his cradle we stand;
   So led by the light of a star sweetly gleaming,
   Here came the wise men from Orient land.
   The king of kings lay thus in lowly manger,
   In all our trials born to be our friend;
   He knows our need, To our weakness is no stranger.
   Behold your King, before Him lowly bend!
   Behold your King, before Him lowly bend!

3. Truly he taught us to love one another;
   His law is love, and His gospel is peace;
   Chains shall he break, for the slave is our brother,
   And in his name all oppression shall cease.
   Sweet hymns of joy in grateful chorus raise we,
   Let all within us praise his holy name;
   Christ is the Lord. Oh, praise his name forever!
   His power and glory evermore proclaim!
   His power and glory evermore proclaim.

Mary's Child

Also known as *Born In The Night* (from the song's opening line)
and penned by a British Methodist preacher, Geoffrey Ainger,
this deceptively simple lyric and tune has found its way into most
modern hymn-song collections for young people.

Born in the Night

Geoffrey Ainger (1925-)

2. Clear shining Light,
   Mary's Child,
   Your face lights up our way;
   Light of the world,
   Mary's Child,
   Dawn on our darkened day.

3. Truth of our life,
   Mary's Child,
   You tell us God is good;
   Prove it is true,
   Mary's Child,
   Go to your Cross of wood.

4. Hope of the world,
   Mary's Child,
   You're coming soon to reign;
   King of the earth,
   Mary's Child,
   Walk in our streets again.

Geoffrey Ainger (1925-   )

Away In A Manger

It has been suggested that Martin Luther was the author of this Christmas hymn, which has become a children's favourite, though adults also enjoy singing it. Edward Heath, the former British Prime Minister, a musician and lover of carols, rightly says In *The Joy Of Christmas* (Sidgwick) that this hymn, when sung to Kirkpatrick's tune, is best rendered with expression and without sentimentality. The same might be said of the American tune which is also given.

FIRST TUNE

Away in a Manger   W.J. Kirkpatrick, 1838-1921

A way in a manger, no crib for a bed, The little Lord Je-sus laid down his sweet head, The stars in the bright sky looked down where he lay, The little Lord Je-sus a-sleep on the hay.

2. The cattle are lowing, the Baby awakes,
   But little Lord Jesus no crying He makes,
   I love Thee, Lord Jesus! Look down from the sky,
   And stay by my side until morning is nigh.

3. Be near me, Lord Jesus; I ask Thee to stay
   Close by me for ever, and love me, I pray.
   Bless all the dear children in Thy tender care,
   And fit us for heaven, to live with Thee there.

Anonymous

62

SECOND TUNE

Mueller

James R. Murray, 1887

A - way in a man - ger, no crib for a bed, The lit - tle Lord

Je - sus laid down his sweet head, The stars in the bright sky looked

down where he lay, The lit - tle Lord Je - sus a - sleep on the hay.

Angels From The Realms Of Glory

Montgomery wrote 400 to 500 hymns and this is regarded as one of his finest lyrics. He commands angels, shepherds, sages and saints to give the respect due, for Christ (Greek: *Christos,* 'the anointed') is the Messiah, the long-awaited king and deliverer. This king, though, is to rule by serving others. Love and goodwill are his active principles and no person is denied the chance of belonging to his kingdom.

Iris

French Carol Melody

An - gels from the realms of glo - ry, Wing your flight o'er all the earth,

Ye, who sang cre - at - ion's sto - ry, Now pro - claim Mes - si - ah's birth;

Come - - and wor - ship

Come - - and

Christ, the new - born King Come -

Come -

and wor - ship, Wor-ship Christ the new - born King,

and

2. Shepherds in the field abiding,
    Watching o'er your flocks by night,
  God with man is now residing,
    Yonder shines the infant light;
      Come and worship.
    Worship Christ, the new-born King.

3. Sages, leave your contemplations;
    Brighter visions beam afar;
  Seek the great Desire of nations;
    Ye have seen His natal star:
      Come and worship,
    Worship Christ, the new-born King.

4. Saints, before the altar bending,
    Watching long with hope and fear,
  Suddenly the Lord, descending,
    In His temple shall appear;
      Come and worship,
    Worship Christ, the new-born King.

James Montgomery, 1771-1854

O Little Town Of Bethlehem

Phillips Brooks wrote his popular hymn at the right
place – Bethlehem. He did so on Christmas Day, 1866. An
American, he was born at Boston, in 1835, and two years before
his death in 1891 he became Protestant Episcopal Bishop of
Massachusetts. Bethlehem comes from Hebrew and Aramaic
words meaning 'house of bread'. Micah 5 verse 2 foretold
Bethlehem as the place where the Messiah would be born.

St. Louis   Lewis H. Redner, 1868

O lit-tle town of Beth-le-hem, How still we _ see thee lie; a-bove thy deep and
dream-less sleep The si-lent _ stars go by. Yet in thy dark streets shin-eth The
ev-er-last-ing Light, The hopes and fears of all the years are met in thee to-night.

2. O morning stars, together
   Proclaim the holy birth,
   And praises sing to God the King,
   And peace to men on earth;
   For Christ is born of Mary;
   And, gathered all above,
   While mortals sleep, the angels keep
   Their watchful wondering love.

3. How silently, how silently
   The wondrous gift is given!
 So God imparts to human hearts
   The blessings of His heaven.
 No ear may hear His coming;
   But in this world of sin,
 Where meek souls will receive Him, still
   The dear Christ enters in.

4. O holy child of Bethlehem,
   Descend to us, we pray;
 Cast out our sin, and enter in;
   Be born in us today.
 We hear the Christmas angels
   The great glad tidings tell;
 O come to us, abide with us,
   Our Lord Immanuel.
         Amen.

Phillips Brooks, 1835-93

All My Heart This Night Rejoices

Lutheran pastor Paulus Gerhardt saw four of his children die in early youth. His wife died after a long illness. And yet this hymn, like others of his, has a joyous carefree stamp upon it. He knows the freedom Jesus offers and gives. He echoes the words of Paul 'To live is to Christ, to die is gain' in his last stanza.

Bonn

J.G. Eberling, 1637-76

All my heart this night re-joic - es, As I hear, far and near,

sweet - est an - gel voi - ces: Christ is born! their choirs are sing -

ing, Till the air, ev - 'ry - where Now with joy is ring - ing.

2. Hark! a voice from yonder manger,
Soft and sweet, doth entreat:
Flee from woe and danger;
Brethren come; from all that doth grieve you,
You are freed; all you need
I will surely give you.

3. Come then, let us hasten yonder;
    Here let all, great and small,
        Kneel in awe and wonder.
 Love Him who with love is yearning;
    Hail the Star, that from far
        Bright with hope is burning.

4. Thee, O Lord, with heed I'll cherish,
    Live to Thee, and with Thee
        Dying, shall not perish,
 But shall dwell with Thee for ever
    Far on high, in the joy
        That can alter never.

Paulus Gerhardt, 1607-76;
tr. by Catherine Winkworth, 1827-78

See Him A-Lying

Michael Perry's calypso carol has become a firm favourite in youth circles. Perry is a clergyman, both Rector of Eversley and Chaplain to the Police Staff College, Bramshill, England. Amidst the outward trappings of physical ordinariness there were at Bethlehem sights, sounds, smells and symbols of a new humanity – a new age for the asking. A baby calls from all people instincts of love but this child bore the title of Saviour the oldest name in our language, which means rescue, cure, healing.

Calypso Carol

Words and Melody: M.A. Perry,
arr. S.K. Coates

See Him a-ly-ing on a bed of straw; _ A draught-y sta-ble with an o-pen door, _

Ma-ry cra-dl-ing the babe she bore; _ The Prince of glo-ry is His name. _

O now car-ry me to Beth-le-hem _ To see the Lord _ ap-pear to men:

To Coda ⊕ *(last verse)*

Just as poor _ as was the sta-ble then _ The Prince of Glo-ry when He came _

The Prince of Glo - ry when He came. _____

2. Star of silver sweep across the skies,
   Show where Jesus in the manger lies,
   Shepherds swiftly from your stupor rise
   To see the Saviour of the world.

3. Angels, sing again the song you sang,
   Bring God's glory to the heart of man:
   Sing that Bethlehem's little Baby can
   Be salvation to the soul.

4. Mine are riches — from thy poverty:
   From thine innocence, eternity;
   Mine, forgiveness by thy death for me,
   Child of sorrow for my joy.

Michael Perry (1942-   )

See Amid The Winter Snow

Indeed, holy and happy is the day on which Christ was born.
No day since can be the same. In this child we see God's total
identification with all mankind. Caswall was for a time an
Anglican vicar, but at the age of 33 he was received into the
Roman Catholic Church. He became a great friend of Cardinal
Newman. He is revered by hymnologists for his translations
of Latin hymns. Composer John Goss was organist at St. Paul's
Cathedral; few tunes have such a vigorous chorus as this
splendid one.

Oxford   *J. Goss, 1800-80*

See, a-mid the win-ter's snow, Born for us on earth be-low, See, the lamb of
God ap-pears, Prom-ised from e - ter - nal years. Hail, thou ev - er bless - ed morn!
Hail, re-demp-tion's hap-py dawn! Sing through all Je - ru - sa-lem: Christ is born in Beth-le-hem!

2. Lo, within a manger lies
   He who built the starry skies,
   He who, throned in height sublime,
   Sits amid the cherubim.

3. Say, ye holy shepherds, say,
   What your joyful news today;
   Wherefore have ye left your sheep
   On the lonely mountain steep?

4. As we watched at dead of night,
   Lo, we saw a wondrous light:
   Angels, singing peace on earth,
   Told us of the Saviour's birth.

5. Sacred Infant, all divine,
   What a tender love was Thine,
   Thus to come from highest bliss
   Down to such a world as this!

6. Teach, O teach us, holy Child,
   By Thy face so meek and mild,
   Teach us to resemble Thee
   In Thy sweet humility.

Edward Caswall, 1814-78

God Rest Ye Merry Gentlemen

Not surprisingly, considering the robust and hearty nature of
the tune, this carol was a great favourite of 19th century
street singers. It must have warmed many a physical frame with
its relentless pace. Another fine tune and different words can
be found in the *Oxford Book of Carols,* number 11. The
mentioned volume notes 'God rest you merry' means 'God keep
you merry'.

English melody, 18th century

God rest you mer-ry, gen-tle-men, Let no-thing you dis - may, Re -

mem-ber Christ our Sa - viour Was born on Christ-mas Day; To save us all from

REFRAIN

Sa-tan's power When we were gone as-tray O ___ ti-dings of com-fort and

joy, com-fort and joy; O ___ ti - dings of com - fort and joy.

2. In Bethlehem in Jewry,
    This blessèd Babe was born,
  And laid within a manger,
    Upon this blessèd morn
  The which His Mother Mary
    Did nothing take in scorn.
      O tidings, etc.

3. From God our Heavenly Father,
    A blessed angel came;
  And unto certain Shepherds
    Brought tidings of the same,
  How that in Bethlehem was born
    The Son of God by name.
      O tidings, etc.

4. "Fear not then," said the Angel,
    "Let nothing you affright,
  This day is born a Saviour
    Of a pure Virgin bright,
  To free all those that trust in Him,
    From Satan's power and might."
      O tidings, etc.

5. The shepherds at these tidings
    Rejoicèd much in mind,
  And left their flocks a-feeding
    In tempest, storm and wind:
  And went to Bethlehem, straightway
    The Son of God to find.
      O tidings, etc.

6. And when they came to Bethlehem,
    Where our dear Saviour lay,
  They found Him in a manger,
    Where oxen fed on hay,
  His Mother Mary kneeling down
    Unto the Lord did pray.
      O tidings, etc.

7. Now to the Lord sing praises,
    All you within this place
  And with true love and brotherhood
    Each other now embrace.
  This holy tide of Christmas
    All other do deface.
      O tidings, etc.

Therefore, with all angels and archangels
And tongues of computers
We give thanks to the romping God
Who through impossibility
Hath delivered us
Into the madness and gladness
Of sure knowledge and salvation.

Chad Walsh

It was a night in winter,
Man and beast asleep,
When Jesus poor and humble,
Did his vigil keep.
The Lord whom kings and prophets
Lovingly foretold,
Lies trembling in a stable,
Dark and bitter cold.
Is this the only welcome,
Saviour at your birth?
In loneliness and sadness
All you find on earth?

Slovak Carol

The people who walked in darkness
have seen a great light;
Upon those who dwelt in the land of gloom
a light has shone.
You have brought them abundant joy
and great rejoicing.

Isaiah 9:2-3

On Christmas night all Christians sing,
To hear the news the angels bring,
On Christmas night all Christians sing
To hear the news the angels bring
News of great joy, news of great mirth
News of our merciful King's birth.

(Sussex Carol, traditional)

Rejoice and be merry in songs and in mirth!
O praise our Redeemer, all mortals on earth!
For this is the birthday of Jesus our King
Who brought us salvation — his praises we'll sing!

A Gallery Carol

The Word becomes incarnate
And yet remains on high!
And Cherubim sing anthems
To shepherds, from the sky:

While thus they sing your Monarch,
These bright angelic bands,
Rejoice, ye vales and mountains,
Ye oceans, clap your hands:

A Great And Mighty Wonder.
St. Germanus

All glory for this blessed morn
To God the Father ever be;
All praise to thee, O Virgin-born,
All praise, O Holy Ghost, to thee.
Amen.

Caelius Sedulius,
tr. John Ellerton

Fairer than the sun at morning

Fairer than the sun at morning
Was the star that told his birth:
To the world its God announcing,
Seen in fleshly form on earth.

Prudentius,
tr. Edward Caswall

A Christmas Carol

Hark now fond heart for 'tis the
gladsome song,
Which greets the coming of a glorious
day,
Hark how the bells ring out in joyous tones,
To tell us 'tis the eve eve Christ
was born

And so he takes her hand within
his own,
And tells of how the bells
once rang for them
A song that lingers still within
his heart,
And marks the advent
of another year.

Then to the casement let thy footsteps glide,
And gaze upon the old familiar scene,
With thoughts of love for those so far
away,
Wishing them all a joyous Christmas-tide.

From an
old MS

Once In Royal David's City

Cecil Frances Alexander was regarded as the 'children's hymnist' of the 19th century. Her hymns and poems totalled around 400 and her volume *Hymns For Little Children* achieved the rare distinction of a hundredth edition. The volume contained *Once In Royal David's City* which was based on the Credal words, 'Who was conceived of the Holy Ghost, born of the Virgin Mary.' Among her other classics are *There Is A Green Hill Far Away* and *All Things Bright And Beautiful*.

2. He came down to earth from heaven
    Who is God and Lord of all,
  And his shelter was a stable,
    And his cradle was a stall;
  With the poor and mean and lowly
  Lived on earth our Saviour holy.

3. And through all his wondrous childhood
    He would honour and obey,
  Love and watch the lowly Maiden,
    In whose gentle arms he lay.
  Christian children all must be,
  Mild, obedient, good as he.

4. And our eyes at last shall see him,
    Through his own redeeming love,
  For that Child so dear and gentle
    Is our Lord in heaven above;
  And he leads his children on
  To the place where he is gone.

5. Not in that poor lowly stable,
    With the oxen standing by,
  We shall see him; but in heaven,
    Set at God's right hand on high;
  Where like stars his children crowned
  All in white shall wait around.

Coventry Carol

This poignant and beautiful carol was sung in the Coventry plays from the 15th century onwards. It tells of Herod's wrath and how he, fearing for his throne, orders the killing of all baby boys. Worthy of close attention is the sadness, implicit in both lyric and music, for the mothers who will lose their sons. It makes a vivid contrast when set against the joy of both family and onlookers who gathered at Bethlehem's manger stall.

Pageant of the Shearmen and Tailors, 15th century

Modern version of tune (M.S.)

Lul - ly, lul - la, thou lit - tle ti - ny child. By by, lul -

ly lul - lay.

1. O sis - ters too, How may we do
2. He - rod, the king, In his rag - ing,
3. That woe is me, Poor child for thee!

For to pre - serve this day This poor young - ling, ___ For
Char - ged he hath this day His men of might, ___ In
And e - ver morn and day, For thy part - ing Nei - ther

After 3rd verse, sing Refrain again

Whom	we	do	sing,	By	by,	lul	-	ly	lul	-	lay?
his	own	sight,		All	young	chil	-	dren	to	-	slay.
say	nor	sing		By	by,	lul	-	ly	lul	-	lay!

D.S.

Born On Earth The Divine Christ Child

A traditional French carol from Normandy, which is becoming
increasingly and deservedly known. A number of lyric
translations exist and the version utilised here comes from *Eight
Christmas Carols* (OUP). Oboes and bagpipes are singled out as
means of giving praise; so also the human voice. 'Rejoice' is the
operative word. And who, other than Puritans of old, could
object to the happy sentiments of this refreshing carol?

English words by
Jacqueline Froom

French traditional carol.
Arranged by Brian Coleman

Born on earth the di-vine Christ-child, O-boes, re-joice with bag-pipes vy-ing, Born on earth the di-vine Christ-child,

sing to wel-come the Sa-viour mild. 'Tis four thou-sand years and more men his birth have been pro-phe-sy-ing,

poco rall.   *a tempo*

'Tis four thou-sand years and more while we longed for the joys in store. Born on earth the di-vine Christ-child,

o-boes, re-joice with bag-pipes vy-ing Born on earth the di-vine Christ-child, sing to wel-come the Sa-viour mild.

2. Ah! such beauty and charm adore!
   Ah! such perfection of grace undying!
   Ah such beauty and charm adore,
   Promised us in days of yore.

   Born on earth the divine Christ-child,
   Oboes, rejoice with bagpipes vying;
   Born on earth the divine Christ-child,
   Sing to welcome the Saviour mild.

3. In a stable here on earth,
   Jesus in the manger lying,
   In a stable here on earth,
   O how lovely our Saviour's birth!

4. Jesus, Saviour, heaven's Lord,
   Tiny child in the manger crying
   Jesus Saviour, heaven's Lord,
   Christ our king for evermore.

English words by Jacqueline Froom

Silent Night

December 24, 1818 saw the first public performance of *Silent Night* in the Church of St. Nikola, in the small town of Oberndorf, near Salzburg, Austria. The lyricist Joseph Mohr was the young priest and Franz Gruber (the composer), the village schoolteacher and church organist. The first music was scored for two male voices, tenor and baritone, guitar accompaniment and a small children's choir. There is now a Silent Night Chapel in Hallein, Austria, and in Oberndorf is the Silent Night Memorial Chapel.

F. Gruber, 1787-1863;
arr. P. Faber, 1947-

Stille Nacht

Si - lent night, ho - ly night, All is calm, all is bright,

round yon vir - gin mo-ther and child. Ho - ly in-fant so ten-der and mild,

sleep in hea-ven-ly peace _____ sleep __ in hea-ven-ly peace.

2. Silent night, holy night.
Shepherds quake at the sight.
Glories stream from heaven afar,
Heavenly hosts sing 'Alleluia!
Christ, the Saviour is born!
Christ, the Saviour is born!'

3. Silent night, holy night,
Son of God, love's pure light:
Radiance beams from thy holy face
With the dawn of redeeming grace,
Jesus, Lord, at thy birth,
Jesus, Lord, at thy birth.

Josef Mohr, 1792-1848;
tr. J. Young

Hark The Herald Angels Sing

The religious truths which burned through Charles Wesley's
mind and body found outlet in over 5,000 hymns. The majestic
theological masterpiece must rate high in his all-time top ten!
Here he explores the basic premise that the coming of Christ was
'the' event in history which discloses the meaning and goal of
human life and living.

Berlin

Mendelssohn, 1809-47

2. Christ, by highest heaven adored,
   Christ, the everlasting Lord,
   Late in time behold him come,
   Offspring of a virgin's womb!
   Veiled in flesh the Godhead see;
   Hail the incarnate Deity!
   Pleased as man with men to dwell,
   Jesus, our Immanuel.

3. Mild He lays his glory by,
   Born that man no more may die,
   Born to raise the sons of earth,
   Born to give them second birth,
   Hail the heaven-born Prince of Peace!
   Hail the Sun of Righteousness!
   Light and life to all he brings,
   Risen with healing in his wings.

Charles Wesley, 1707-88

While Shepherds Watched

Scripture makes much of 'shepherds' and 'sheep' and so it is not surprising that 'shepherds' were among the first to hear the good news of Jesus's impending birth. Psalm 23 stands pre-eminent in exploring God's mercies in terms of the 'shepherd' and 'sheep' while John 10:11, Isaiah 40:11, Ezekiel 1:16, 34:11-16, Psalms 78:70-72 are among other celebrated references. Some shepherds were nomads, others lived in villages such as Beit Sahur, close to Bethlehem. Nahum Tate was born in Dublin and he became Poet Laureate in 1692. He died in London. Two tunes are given below. Another useful one is Northrop.

FIRST TUNE

Winchester Old   *G. Kirbye (?), 1634*

2. Fear not! said he; for mighty dread
   Had seized their troubled mind:
   Glad tidings of great joy I bring
   To you and all mankind.

3. To you, in David's town, this day
   Is born of David's line,
   A Saviour, who is Christ the Lord;
   And this shall be the sign:

4. The heavenly Babe you there shall find
   To human view displayed,
   All meanly wrapped in swaddling bands
   And in a manger laid.

5. Thus spake the seraph; and forthwith
   Appeared a shining throng
   Of angels praising God, and thus
   Addressed their joyful song:

6. All glory be to God on high,
   And to the earth be peace;
   Good will henceforth from heaven to men
   Begin and never cease!
   Amen.

   Nahum Tate, 1652-1715

SECOND TUNE

Lyngham   T. Jarman, 1776-1861

While shep-herds watched their flocks by night, All seat-ed on the

ground, All seat - ed on the ground, The an-gel of the

Lord came down,   And glo-ry shone a-

And glo - ry shone a - round   And glo-ry shone a -

And glo - ry shone a - round,   And   glo - ry shone a - round.

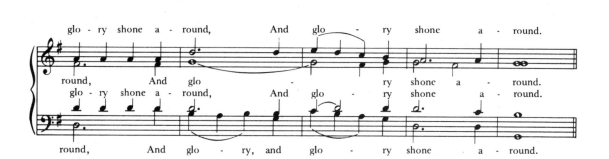

glo - ry shone a - round,   And glo - ry shone a - round.

round,   And glo   -   ry shone a - round.

glo - ry shone a - round,   And glo - ry shone a - round.

round,   And glo - ry, and glo - ry shone a - round.

We Three Kings

A splendid 19th century North American carol which is made
for dramatic presentation and more than most carols it
instinctively suggests rich and colourful scenes. Whether the
Wise Men of Scripture were 'kings' is doubtful, as is the later
story which suggests the 'kings' were named Gaspar, Melchior
and Balthasar.

Kings of Orient

J.H. Hopkins, Jr. 1857

We three kings of o-ri-ent are; Bear-ing gifts we tra-verse a-far,

Field and foun-tain, moor and moun-tain, fol-low-ing yon-der star.

REFRAIN

O____ star of won-der, star of night, Star with roy-al beau-ty bright,

west-ward lead-ing still pro-ceed-ing, guide us to thy per-fect light.

2. Born a king on Bethlehem plain,
   Gold I bring, to crown him again.
   King for ever, ceasing never,
   Over us all to reign:

   O star of wonder, star of night,
   Star with royal beauty bright,
   Westward leading, still proceeding,
   Guide us to thy perfect light.

3. Frankincense to offer have I;
   Incense owns a Deity nigh:
   Prayer and praising, all men raising,
   Worship him, God most high:

4. Myrrh is mine; its bitter perfume
   Breathes a life of gathering gloom,
   Sorrowing, sighing, bleeding, dying,
   Sealed in the stone-cold tomb:

5. Glorious now, behold him arise,
   King, and God, and sacrifice!
   Heaven sings alleluya,
   Alleluya the earth replies:

As With Gladness

William Chatterton Dix wrote his Epiphany hymn for use at
St. Raphael's, Bristol. It seems that he was recovering from
serious illness in 1860 when the shape of this hymn came to
mind and the lines were transmitted to paper. The 'wise men'
were most likely stargazers who, conversant with astrology and
magic, believed that the emergence of a new star denoted the
coming of a great world leader.

Dix

C. Kocher, 1786-1872

As with glad-ness men of old Did the guid-ing star be-hold,

As with joy they hailed its light, Lead-ing on-ward, beam-ing bright;

So, most grac-ious Lord, may we Ev-er-more be led to Thee.

2. As with joyful steps they sped,
   Saviour, to Thy lowly bed,
   There to bend the knee before
   Thee, whom heaven and earth adore;
   So may we with willing feet
   Ever seek the mercy-seat.

3. As they offered gifts most rare
   At Thy cradle rude and bare;
   So may we with holy joy,
   Pure, and free from sin's alloy,
   All our costliest treasures bring,
   Christ, to Thee, our heavenly King.

4. Holy Jesus, every day
   Keep us in the narrow way;
   And, when earthly things are past,
   Bring our ransomed souls at last
   Where they need no star to guide,
   Where no clouds Thy glory hide.

5. In the heavenly country bright
   Need they no created light;
   Thou its light, its joy, its crown,
   Thou its sun which goes not down;
   There for ever may we sing
   Hallelujahs to our King.

   William Chatterton Dix, 1837-98

93

Jesus Jesus Rest Your Head

A (North American) Southern Appalachian carol which deserves
to be more generally known. In attractive simplicity it both asks
a question amd makes a statement. Nothing is known of either
the lyric or music writers.

1. Have you heard a - bout our Je - sus? Have you heard a - bout His fate?
2. To the man - ger came the Wise Men, Bring - ing gifts un - to the Son;

How His mam - my went to the sta - ble On that Christ - mas Eve so late?
Saw the mo - ther and the fa - ther And the lit - tle bles - sed One.

molto legato
Winds were blow - ing o - xen low - ing, Stars were glow - ing,

Dal.%.
(a tempo e senza pausa)
molto rall. e dim.

Winds were blowing ing, Stars were glow - ing, glow - ing.

molto legato

molto rall. e dim.

Who Is He In Yonder Stall

Simple and effective, this hymn by an American minister and
first located in *The Dove: A Collection Of Music For Day And
Sunday-schools,* Chicago, 1866, traces the steps of Jesus from
birth to ascension.

Who is he?

B.R. Hanby, 1833-67
CHORUS

Who is He, in yon-der stall, At those feet the shep-herds fall? 'Tis the
Lord! O wond-rous sto-ry! 'Tis the Lord, the King of glo-ry! At his
feet we humb-ly fall, Crown Him, Crown Him Lord of all.

2. Who is he, in yonder cot,
   Bending to his toilsome lot?

3. Who is He, in deep distress,
   Fasting in the wilderness?

4. Who is He that stands and weeps
   At the grave where Lazarus sleeps?

5. Lo, at midnight, who is He
   Prays in dark Gethsemane?

6. Who is He, in Calvary's throes,
   Asks for blessings on his foes?

7. Who is He that from the grave
   Comes to heal and help and save?

8. Who is He that from His throne
   Rules through all the worlds alone?

Benjamin Russell Hanby, 1833-67

Cheer Up Freinds

N.S.T

French
(M.S.)

Moderately quick

1. Cheer___ up, friends and neigh - bours, Now___ it's East - er___ tide;
2. Out___ from snow - drifts chil - ly, Roused___ from drow - sy___ hours;

Stop___ from end - less la - bours, Wor - ries put a - side:
Blue - bell wakes, and li - ly; God___ calls up the___ flowers!

Men___ should rise from sad - ness, E - vil, fol - ly,___ strife,
In - to life he rais - es All___ the sleep - ing___ buds;

When___ God's might - y glad - ness Brings___ the earth to life.
Mea - dows weave his prais - es, And___ the spang - led woods.

3. All his truth and beauty,
   All his righteousness,
   Are our joy and duty,
   Bearing his impress:
   Look! the earth waits breathless
   After winter's strife:
   Easter shows man deathless,
   Spring leads death to life.

4. Ours the more and less is;
   But, changeless all the days,
   God revives and blesses,
   Like the sunlight rays.
   'All mankind is risen.'
   The Easter bells do ring.
   While from out their prison
   Creep the flowers of spring!

French (M.S.)

Remember O Thou Man

Probably 16th century, the words are set to music in
Ravenscroft's Melismata. Thomas Hardy gives another version in
Under the Greenwood Tree.

Melismata, 1611

*Ibid
(Thomas Ravenscroft, 1611)*

1. Re - mem - ber, O thou man, O thou man, O thou man, Re - mem - ber,
2. Re - mem - ber, God's good - ness, O thou man, O thou man, Re - mem - ber,

O thou man, Thy time is spent: Re - mem - ber, O thou man,
God's good - ness And pro - mise made: Re - mem - ber God's good - ness,

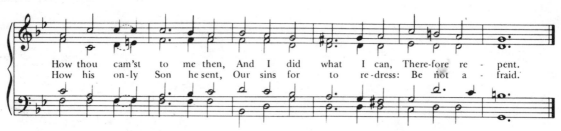

How thou cam'st to me then, And I did what I can, There-fore re - pent.
How his on - ly Son he sent, Our sins for to re - dress: Be not a - fraid.

3. The angels all did sing,
   O thou man, O thou man,
   The angels all did sing,
   On Sion hill:
   The angels all did sing
   Praises to our heavenly King,
   And peace to man living,
   With right good will.

4. To Bethlem did they go,
   O thou man, O thou man,
   To Bethlem did they go,
   This thing to see:
   To Bethlem did they go,
   To see whether it was so,
   Whether Christ was born or no
   To set us free.

5. In Bethlem was he born,
   O thou man, O thou man,
   In Bethlem was he born,
   For mankind dear:
   In Bethlem was he born
   For us that were forlorn,
   And therefore took no scorn,
   Our sins to bear.

6. Give thanks to God always,
   O thou man, O thou man,
   Give thanks to God always,
   With hearts most jolly:
   Give thanks to God always
   Upon this blessed day;
   Let all men sing and say,
   Holy, holy.

Thomas Ravenscroft, 1611

The Strife Is O'Er

12th century, translated in the 17th from Symphonia Sirenum,
Cologne, by Francis Pott, who was Rector of Norhill, Ely,
1866-91. Among his other best known works are *Forty Days And
Forty Nights* and *Lift Up Your Heads, Eternal Gates.*

*First three lines adapted from
a Gloria Patri by G.P. da Palestrina, 1525-94
Alleluia by W.H. Monk*

The strife is o'er, the bat - tle done; Now is the Vic - tor's 'tri - umph
won; Now be the song of praise be - gun: Al - le - lu - ia!

2. The powers of death have done their worst,
   But Christ their legions hath dispersed;
   Let shouts of holy joy outburst:
     Alleluia!

3. The three sad days have quickly sped;
   He rises glorious from the dead;
   All glory to our risen Head:
     Alleluia!

4. Lord, by the stripes which wounded Thee,
   From death's dread sting Thy servants free,
   That we may live and sing to Thee:
     Alleluia!

*Anonymous, c. 12th century,
tr. from Symphonia Sirenum,
Cologne, 1695,
by Francis Pott, 1832-1909*

O mortal man, remember well,
When Christ our Lord was born
He was crucified between two thieves
And crowned with the thorn.

Sussex, Mummer's Carol

O praise to him who came to save,
Who conquered death and burst the grave;
Each day new praise resoundeth
To him the Lamb who once was slain,
The friend who none shall trust in vain,
Whose grace for aye aboundeth;
Sing, ye heavens, tell the story,
　　Of his glory,
　　Till his praises
Flood with light earth's darkest places!

Philipp Nicolai, Johann Schlegel.
Tr: Catherine Winksworth

The king of all power was in Bethlehem born.
Who wore for our sakes a crown of thorn.
Then God preserve us both even and morn
For Jesus' sake, our dearest dear!

Joseph and Mary, Traditional Carol

Let us now in every nation
Sing his praise with exultation.
All the world shall find salvation
In the birth of Mary's Son.

Shepherds Left Their Flock
A Straying.
Imogen Holst

Come, my beloved,
Let us walk among the little hills,
for the snows have melted
and life is awakened from its sleep
and wanders through the hills
and valleys.

Come, let us follow
the footsteps of Spring
in the far-off field;
Come and we will ascend the heights
and look upon
the waving greenness
of the plains below.

Kahlil Gibran
from A Tear And A Smile
© Alfred A. Knopf

Love Is Come Again

Louis Savary S.J. has written: 'If Easter love is hurt, it forgives.
If love in Spring does any harm, it is quick to set things right
again. Springtime is Easter when love rises from the earth, never
again to be broken or destroyed.'

J.M.C. Crum

French
(M.S.)

In moderate time

1. Now the green blade ris - eth from the bur - ied grain, Wheat that in
2. In the grave they laid him, Love whom men had slain, Think - ing that

dark earth ma - ny days has lain; Love lives a - gain, that
nev - er he would wake a - gain, Laid in the earth like

with the dead has been: Love is come a - gain, Like wheat that spring-eth green.
grain that sleeps un - seen: Love is come a - gain, Like wheat that spring-eth green.

3. Forth he came at Easter, like the risen grain,
   He that for three days in the grave had lain,
   Quick from the dead my risen Lord is seen:
       Love is come again, etc.

4. When our hearts are wintry, grieving, or in pain,
   Thy touch can call us back to life again,
   Fields of our hearts that dead and bare have been:
       Love is come again, etc.

                            French (M.S.)

The Gospel Bells Are Ringing

A familiar song to those who are conversant with Ira D. Sankey's
Sacred Songs and Solos. He was soloist at the large-scale
revival meetings conducted by American evangelist Daniel L.
Moody. Moody argued for no doctrine but one, 'Believe in the
Lord Jesus Christ and thou shalt be saved,' convicted of
sin by the influence of the Holy Spirit, saved by faith in
the redeeming blood of the Saviour.

S. Wesley Martin

The Gos-pel bells are ring-ing ov-er land, from sea to sea; Bles-sed news of free sal-

va-tion Do they of-fer you and me. "For God so loved the world That His on-ly Son He

CHORUS
Gos-pel
gave Who-so-e'er be-liev-eth in Him Ev-er-last-ing life shall have."

bells,   how they ring!   Gos-pel
Gos-pel bells,   how they ring! Ov-er land from sea to sea;

2. The gospel bells invite us
   To a feast prepared for all;
   Do not slight the invitation,
   Nor reject the gracious call.
   "I am the bread of life;
   Eat of me, thou hungry soul;
   Though your sins be red as crimson,
   They shall be as white as snow."

3. The gospel bells are joyful,
   As they echo far and wide,
   Bearing notes of perfect pardon,
   Through a Saviour crucified.
   "Good tidings of great joy
   To all people do I bring;
   Unto you is born a Saviour,
   Which is Christ the Lord" and King.

   S. Wesley Martin

When I Survey The Wondrous Cross

Dr. Eric Routley, the renowned hymnologist, says this is
the most penetrating of all hymns, the most demanding,
the most imaginative. He adds: 'It is these things precisely
because its style is so simple. It is drawn throughout in strong,
clear, simple lines and colours.' The scriptural base
is Galatians 6:14.

FIRST TUNE

Rockingham   *Adapted by E. Miller, 1731-1807*

When I survey the wond-'rous Cross On which the
Prince of Glo-ry died, My rich-est gain I count but
loss, And pour con-tempt on all my pride.

2. Forbid it, Lord, that I should boast,
　　Save in the death of Christ, my God:
　　All the vain things that charm me most,
　　　I sacrifice them to His blood.

3. See, from His head, His hands, His feet,
　　Sorrow and love flow mingled down:
　　Did e'er such love and sorrow meet,
　　　Or thorns compose so rich a crown?

4. Were the whole realm of nature mine,
　　That were an offering far too small;
　　Love so amazing, so divine,
　　　Demands my soul, my life, my all.

Isaac Watts, 1674-1748

SECOND TUNE

Boston   *L. Mason*

When I sur-vey the___ wond-'rous___ Cross   on   which the Prince of___ Glo - ry___ died,

My   rich-est gain I ___ count but___ loss,   And pour con-tempt on   all   my___ pride.

Man Of Sorrows

Writer Philipp Bliss was born at Clearfield, Pennsylvania,
U.S.A. In 1874 he announced that he would give the royalties of
his *Gospel Songs,* worth $30,000, to evangelical work. Sadly, he
died two years later in the railway disaster at Ashtabula, Ohio.
He had escaped from the burning railway carriage, but lost his
life in trying to rescue his wife. Among his other well-known
hymns is *Hold The Fort,* a familiar closing hymn at the mission
meetings of Daniel L. Moody.

Gethsemane   *P. Bliss, 1838-76*

Man of Sor-rows! What a name___ For the Son of God, who came

Ru - ined sin - ners to re - claim! Hal - le - lu - jah! What a Sav - iour!

2. Bearing shame and scoffing rude,
   In my place condemned He stood;
   Sealed my pardon with His blood:
   Hallelujah! what a Saviour!

3. Guilty, vile, and helpless we;
   Spotless Lamb of God was He:
   Full atonement — can it be?
   Hallelujah! what a Saviour!

4. Lifted up was He to die.
   It is finished! was His cry;
   Now in heaven exalted high:
   Hallelujah! what a Saviour!

5. When He comes, our glorious King,
   All His ransomed home to bring,
   Then anew this song we'll sing:
   Hallelujah! what a Saviour!

Philipp Bliss, 1838-76

Jesus Keep Me Near The Cross

One of many hymns which were written by Frances Jane van Alstyne, a lady better known simply as Fanny Crosby. She was born at South East, Putney Country, New York and was blind from six weeks old.

Near the Cross

W.H. Doane, 1832-1916

Je - sus, keep me near the Cross; There a prec - ious foun - tain,

Free to all, a heal - ing stream, Flows from Cal - vary's moun - tain.

CHORUS

In the Cross, in the Cross, Be my glo - ry ev - er;

Till my rap - tured soul shall find Rest be - yond the riv - er.

2. Near the Cross, a trembling soul,
   Love and mercy found me;
   There the bright and morning star
   Shed its beams around me.

3. Near the Cross: O Lamb of God,
   Bring its scenes before me;
   Help me walk from day to day,
   With its shadow o'er me.

4. Near the Cross I'll watch and wait,
   Hoping, trusting ever,
   Till I reach the golden strand,
   Just beyond the river.

Frances Jane van Alstyne,
1820-1915

There Is A Green Hill Far Away

Mrs. Alexander based this famous hymn on 'Suffered under
Pontius Pilate, was crucified, dead and buried' from the
Apostles Creed. As with other hymns of hers, Mrs. Alexander
wrote with the express purpose of answering children's questions
about the Faith. The initial question underlying its sentiments is
Why did Jesus die?

Horsley   *W. Horsley, 1774-1858*

There is a green hill far a - way, With - out a ci - ty wall, Where the dear Lord was cru - ci - fied Who died to save us all.

2. We may not know, we cannot tell
   What pains he had to bear;
   But we believe it was for us
   He hung and suffered there.

3. He died that we might be forgiven,
   He died to make us good,
   That we might at last go to heaven,
   Saved by his precious blood.

4. There was no other good enough
   To pay the price of sin;
   He only could unlock the gate
   Of heaven, and let us in.

5. Oh, dearly, dearly has he loved,
   And we must love him too,
   And trust in his redeeming blood,
   And try his works to do.

Cecil Frances Alexander, 1823-95

O sacred head, once wounded,
With grief and shame weighed down!
O kingly head, surrounded
With thorns, thine only crown!
How pale art thou with anguish!
With sore abuse and scorn!
How does that visage languish,
Which once was bright as morn!

Paul Gerhardt.
Tr: James Waddell Alexander

In the cross of Christ I glory,
Towering all the wrecks of time;
All the light of sacred story
Gathers round its head sublime.

John Bowring

At the cross! at the cross! where I first saw the light,
And the burden of my heart rolled away,
It was there by faith I received my sight,
And now I am happy all the day!

Anonymous

Hymns of praise, then, let us sing
Unto Christ, our heavenly king,
Who endured the cross and grave,
Sinners to redeem and save.
Sing we to our God above
Praise eternal as his love;
Praise him, all ye heavenly host,
Father, Son, and Holy Ghost!
        Amen.

Lyra Davidica

'Glory be to Jesus!'
Let all his children say;
'He rose again, he rose again,
On this glad day!'

John Ellerton

Meditation on the resurrection of Jesus Christ
can help a man not merely to be alive
but to know that he is alive.

Chad Walsh

Blest morning, whose first dawning rays
Beheld the son of God.

Isaac Watts

The Lord of all things lives anew,
And all his works are rising too:
    Hosanna in excelsis!

John Mason Neale

No condemnation now I dread
Jesus, and all in Him, is mine:
Alive in him, my living Head,
And clothed in righteousness divine,
Bold I approach the eternal throne,
And claim the crown, through Christ, my own.

Charles Wesley

O believe the record true,
God to you His son hath given,
Ye may now be happy too,
Live on earth the life of heaven;
Live the life of heaven above,
All the life of glorious love.

Charles Wesley

Christ The Lord Is Risen Today

Hallelujah (praise Jah or Praise ye the Lord) is the order of the
day after each and every line. And no wonder – for see the
staggering claims Wesley makes for the Christ who rose from the
grave. The Resurrected Christ can heal, forgive, change and
bring people together. It says there is a time to live and that
time is always. Hallelujah!

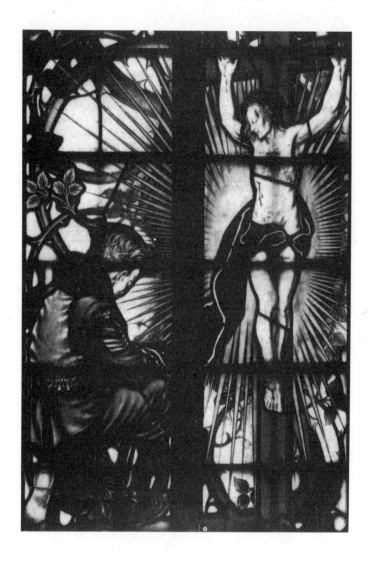

2. Love's redeeming work is done;
   Fought the fight, the battle won:
   Vain the stone, the watch, the seal;
   Christ hath burst the gates of hell:

3. Lives again our glorious King:
   Where, O death, is now thy sting?
   Once He died our souls to save:
   Where's thy victory, boasting grave?

4. Soar we now where Christ hath led,
   Following our exalted Head;
   Made like Him, like Him we rise;
   Ours the cross, the grave, the skies:

5. King of glory! Soul of bliss!
   Everlasting life is this,
   Thee to know, Thy power to prove,
   Thus to sing, and thus to love:

Charles Wesley, 1707-88

A Toi La Gloire O Ressucite

Young people at Taize in the 1970s said the Risen Christ
prepares his people to become at one and the same time a
contemplative people thirsting for God; a people of justice,
living the struggle of men, women, people exploited; a people of
communion, where the non-believer also finds a creative place.
These involved people are friends of the Resurrected Christ.

G.F. Handel, 1746

118

2. See, here is Jesus! Who else could it be?
   He, your Lord and Saviour, surely it is he!
   Happy Church of Jesus, who doubt no more,
   Never cease to tell us Christ is conqueror!
     Yours be the glory, yours O Risen Friend!
     You have won for ever victory without end!

3. He lives for ever! Bids me fear no more;
   He is Prince of Peace, the one whom I adore,
   With him to support me, victory shall be won:
     Yours be the glory, yours O Risen Friend!
     You have won for ever victory without end!

English version by F. Pratt Green

Jesus Lives Thy Terrors Now

Easter is about the mighty act of God. Jesus is raised from the dead. The event stuns the natural senses. It seems impossible. The once dispirited, numbed, heart-broken followers shout, 'It is true!' He did defeat death and now death has no sting.

St. Albinus

H.J. Gauntlett, 1805-76

Je - sus lives! thy ter - rors now Can, O death, no more ap - pal us; Je - sus lives! by this we know Thou, O grave, canst not en - thral us. Hal - le - lu - jah!

2. Jesus lives! to Him the throne
   High o'er heaven and earth is given;
   We may go where He is gone,
   Live and reign with Him in heaven.
   Hallelujah!

3. Jesus lives! for us He died;
   Hence may we, to Jesus living,
   Pure in heart and act abide,
   Praise to Him and glory giving.
   Hallelujah!

4. Jesus lives! our hearts know well
    Nought from us His love shall sever;
  Life, nor death, nor powers of hell,
    Part us now from Christ for ever.
            Hallelujah!

5. Jesus lives! henceforth is death
    Entrance-gate of life immortal;
  This shall calm our trembling breath
    When we pass its gloomy portal.
            Hallelujah!

            Christian Furchtegott Gellert,
                    1715-69;
            tr. by Frances Elizabeth Cox,
                    1812-97

Fair waved the golden corn
In Canaan's pleasant land,
When full of joy, some shining morn,
Went forth the reaper band.

John Hampden Gurney

The golden sunshine, vernal air,
Sweet flowers and fruits thy love declare;
Where harvests ripen, thou art there,
Who givest all.

Christopher Wordsworth

Praise him that he made the sun
Day by day his course to run:
Praise him that he gave the rain
To mature the swelling grain:
And hath bid the fruitful field
Crops of precious increase yield:
Praise him for our harvest store,
He hath filled the garner floor.

Henry Williams Baker

For the beauty of the earth,
For the beauty of the skies,
For the love which from our birth
Over and around us lies,
    Gracious God, to thee we raise
    This our sacrifice of praise.

Folliott Sandford Pierpoint

Autumn is melons and mists, purple grapes that cling to
the vine and cornstalks that soldier the fields. It is
thanksgiving. There is dancing and laughter beneath a
magic orange moon. In autumn the world wears well.

from Listen To Love. *Compiled by Louis Savary*

What has become perfect,
All that is ripe — wants to die.
All that is unripe wants to live.
All that suffers wants to live
That it may become ripe and joyous
And longing — longing for what is
Farther, higher, brighter.

Friedrich Nietzsche

Sing to the Lord of harvest,
Sing songs of love and praise
With joyful hearts and voices
Your hallelujahs raise.

J.S.B. Monsell

All occasions invite his mercies
and all times are his seasons.

John Donne

Honour the Lord with substance,
and with the first fruits of all your increase.
So shall your barns be filled with plenty,
and your presses shall burst out with new wine.

Proverbs 3: 9-10

All Things Bright And Beautiful

Helen Keller once said she had walked with people whose eyes
are full of light, but who see nothing in sea or sky. She added
that it were far better to sail forever in the night of blindness
than to be content with the mere act of seeing. It seems apt
comment in the light of Mrs. Alexander's last verse.

All Things Bright and Beautiful

W.H. Monk, 1823-89

REFRAIN

1. All things bright and beau - ti - ful, all crea - tures great and small,

all things wise and won - der - ful, The Lord God made them all.

2. Each lit - tle flow'r that o - pens, each lit - tle bird that sings, he

made their glow - ing co - - lours, he made their ti - ny wings.

3. The purple-headed mountain,
   The river running by,
   The sunset, and the morning
   That brightens up the sky.

4. The cold wind in the winter,
   The pleasant summer sun,
   The ripe fruits in the garden,
   He made them every one.

5. He gave us eyes to see them,
   And lips, that we might tell
   How great is God almighty,
   Who has made all things well.

Cecil Frances Alexander,
1823-95

We Thank Thee Lord For This Fair Earth

People who love nature but ignore their fellow human beings
receive short shrift from writer George Edward Lynch Cotton.
He was at one time an assistant master at Rugby School and is
'The Young Master' in *Tom Brown's Schooldays*.

Holly   G. Hews, 1806-73

We thank Thee, Lord, for this fair earth, The glitt-'ring sky, the sil-ver sea;

For all their beau-ty, all their worth, Their light and glo-ry come from Thee.

2. Thanks for the flowers that clothe the ground,
   The trees that wave their arms above,
   The hills that gird our dwellings round,
   As Thou dost gird Thine own with love.

3. Yet teach us how still far more fair,
   More glorious, Father in thy sight,
   Is one pure deed, one holy prayer,
   One heart that owns Thy spirit's might.

4. So, while we gaze with thoughtful eye
   On all the gifts Thy love has given,
   Help us in Thee to live and die,
   By Thee to rise from earth to heaven.
                                    Amen.

George Edward Lynch Cotton, 1813-66

We Plough The Fields And Scatter

Matthias Claudius was the son of a Lutheran pastor. Miss
Campbell was a daughter of the manse. Claudius' words first
appeared as part of a sketch, Paul Erdmann's Fest. Miss
Campbell's translation appeared in the Rev. C.S. Bere's *Garland
Of Songs,* 1861. Arguably this is the best known and most used
of harvest hymns.

Wir Pflügen

J.A.P. Schultz, 1747-1800

We plough the fields and scat- ter the good seed on the land, But it is fed and
wat- ered by God's al- might- y hand; He sends the snow in win- ter, the
warmth to swell the grain, The breez-es and the sun- shine, And soft re- fresh-ing rain.

REFRAIN

All good gifts a- round us are sent from heav'n a- bove, Then

thank the Lord, O thank the Lord, For all_____ his love.

2. He only is the Maker
   Of all things near and far;
   He paints the wayside flower,
   He lights the evening star;
   The winds and waves obey Him,
   By Him the birds are fed;
   Much more to us, His children,
   He gives our daily bread.

3. We thank Thee then, O Father,
   For all things bright and good,
   The seed-time and the harvest,
   Our life, our health, our food;
   Accept the gifts we offer
   For all Thy love imparts,
   And, what Thou most desirest,
   Our humble, thankful hearts.
                    Amen.

Matthias Claudius, 1740-1815;
tr. by Jane Montgomery Campbell,
                    1817-78

To Thee O Lord Our Hearts We Raise

A useful processional hymn, *To Thee, O Lord,* was written in 1863. The writer is William Chatterton Dix who penned *As With Gladness Men Of Old.* Verse two, with its reference to 'first fruits', recalls Exodus 23:16, 34:22 and Deuteronomy 18:4 where Hebrew law says the first fruits of harvest and newly sheared wool should be given to the Lord.

Bishopgarth

A. Sullivan, 1842-1900

To Thee, O Lord, our hearts we raise in hymns of a - do - ra - tion, To Thee bring sac - ri - fice of praise With shouts of ex - ul - ta - tion; Bright robes of gold the fields ad - orn, The hills with joy are ring - ing, The val - leys stand so thick with corn That ev - en they are sing - ing.

2. And now, on this our festal day,
   Thy bounteous hand confessing,
Before Thee thankfully we lay
   The first-fruits of Thy blessing.
By Thee the souls of men are fed
   With gifts of grace supernal;
Thou who dost give us earthly bread,
   Give us the bread eternal.

3. We bear the burden of the day,
   And often toil seems dreary;
But labour ends with sunset ray,
   And rest comes for the weary:
May we, the angel-reaping o'er,
   Stand at the last accepted,
Christ's golden sheaves for evermore
   To garners bright elected.

4. O blessed is that land of God
   Where saints abide for ever,
Where golden fields spread far and broad,
   Where flows the crystal river.
The strains of all its holy throng
   With ours today are blending;
Thrice blessèd is that harvest song
   Which never hath an ending.

William Chatterton Dix, 1837-98

Come Ye Thankful People Come

Henry Alford published this popular hymn in his 1844
publication *Psalms And Hymns.* Lord Palmerston made him
Dean of Canterbury in 1857 and he was known for his edition
of the Greek Testament, in four volumes. Alford is the writer
of the one-time popular processional hymn *Forward Be Our
Watchword.* Some would say it is more popular than *We Plough
The Fields* – certainly any preacher who omitted these two
hymns at a harvest gathering might be thought strange and even
foolish.

St. George's, Windsor   *G.J. Elvey, 1816-93*

Come, ye thank-ful peo-ple, come, Raise the song of har-vest home:

All is safe-ly gath-ered in, Ere the win-ter storms be-gin;

God our Ma-ker doth pro-vide For our wants to be sup-plied:

Come to God's own tem-ple, come, Raise the song of har-vest home!

2. All the world is God's own field,
   Fruit unto His praise to yield;
   Wheat and tares together sown,
   Unto joy or sorrow grown;
   First the blade, and then the ear,
   Then the full corn shall appear;
   Grant, O harvest Lord, that we
   Wholesome grain and pure may be.

3. For the Lord our God shall come,
   And shall take His harvest home;
   From His field shall in that day
   All offences purge away;
   Give His angels charge at last
   In the fire the tares to cast;
   But the fruitful ears to store
   In His garner evermore.

4. Even so, Lord, quickly come;
   Bring Thy final harvest home:
   Gather Thou Thy people in,
   Free from sorrow, free from sin;
   There, for ever purified,
   In Thy garner to abide:
   Come, with all Thine angels, come,
   Raise the glorious harvest-home!
                          Amen.

Henry Alford, 1810-71

133

Now The Year Is Crowned With Blessing

Ellen Fowler (Mrs. Felkin by marriage) unlike most harvest
hymn-writers does not stray from harvest of the land to
the harvest of souls at the great Judgement Day. She allows
herself and us to savour the splendours of Autumn, Spring
and Summer.

Morgenlied

F.C. Maker, 1844-1927

Now the year is crowned with bless-ing As we gath-er in the grain; And, our grate-ful
thanks ex-press-ing, Loud we raise a joy-ous strain. By-gone days of toil and sad-ness
Can-not now our peace des-troy; For the hills are clothed with glad-ness, And the val-leys

REFRAIN

shout for joy. To the Lord their first fruits bring-ing All His thank-ful peo-ple come,

To the Fa - ther prais - es sing-ing For the joy of har - vest home.

2. In the spring the smiling meadows
       Donned their robes of living green,
   As the sunshine chased the shadows
       Swiftly o'er the changing scene;
   In the summer-time the story
       Of a riper hope was told;
   Then the rich autumnal glory
       Decked the fields in cloth of gold.

3. Shall not we, whose hearts are swelling
       With the thought of former days,
   Sing a joyous song foretelling
       Future gladness, fuller praise?
   For the cloud the bow retaineth
       With its covenant of peace,
   That, as long as earth remaineth,
       Harvest-time shall never cease.

Ellen Thorneycroft Fowler
(Mrs. Felkin), 1860-1929

Sowing In The Morning

The Christian cannot do as he wishes with no thought of
the consequences. His commitment to Jesus means grasping
new possibilities and new potentialities for people; it's the case
of seeing what God is offering for this moment and acting,
the courage to invest one's life. The sowing of good seed in
the right places will produce fruit.

George A. Miner

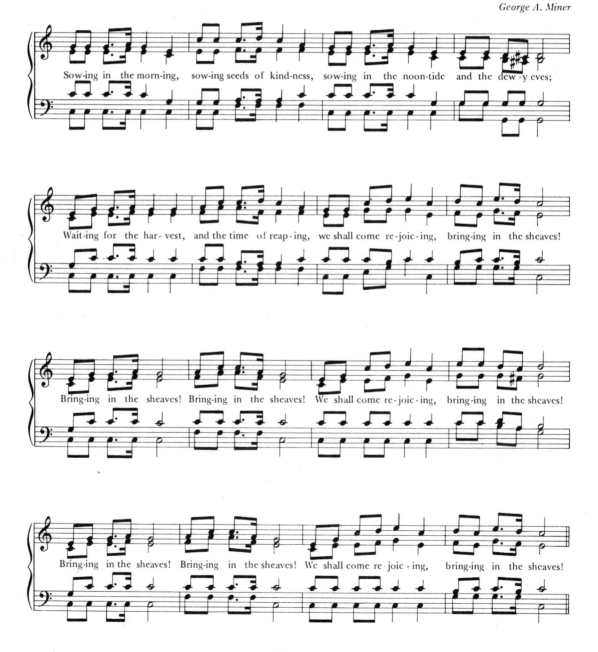

Sow-ing in the morn-ing, sowing seeds of kind-ness, sow-ing in the noon-tide and the dew-y eves;

Wait-ing for the har-vest, and the time of reap-ing, we shall come re-joic-ing, bring-ing in the sheaves!

Bring-ing in the sheaves! Bring-ing in the sheaves! We shall come re-joic-ing, bring-ing in the sheaves!

Bring-ing in the sheaves! Bring-ing in the sheaves! We shall come re-joic-ing, bring-ing in the sheaves!

2. Sowing in the sunshine, sowing in the shadows,
   Fearing neither clouds nor winter's chilling breeze;
   By and by the harvest, and the labour ended,
   We shall come rejoicing, bringing in the sheaves!

3. Go then ever, weeping, sowing for the Master,
   Tho' the loss sustained our spirit often grieves:
   When our weeping's over, He will bid us welcome,
   We shall come rejoicing, bringing in the sheaves!

George A. Miner

137

Some Are Sowing Their Seed

Galatians says clearly: 'Whatsoever a man soweth, that shall
he also reap.' Jesus said 'Feed my sheep' and when he asked
his close followers, particularly Peter, 'Do you love me?' he
was not asking for approval – rather, those who love Jesus will
love others. When this is the case then the harvest will be good.

W.H. Doane

Some are sow - ing their seed in the dawn-light fair, They are sow-ing seed in the
noon-day glare; They are sow-ing seed in the soft twi - light; They are sow - ing their seed in the

CHORUS

sol - emn night. What shall the har - vest be? What shall the har-vest be?

What shall the har - vest be? What shall the har - vest be?

2. Some are sowing their seed of word and deed,
    Which the cold know not, nor the careless heed;
    Oh, the gentle word, and the kindest deed,
    That have blessed the sad heart in its sorest need.
Refrain: Sweet shall the harvest be! (repeat three more times)

3. Some are sowing the seed of noble deed,
    With a sleepless watch and an earnest heed;
    With a ceaseless hand in the earth they sow,
    And the fields are all whit'ning where'er they go.
Refrain: Rich will the harvest be! (repeat three more times)

4. Whether sown in the darkness or sown in the light;
    Whether sown in weakness, or sown in might;
    Whether sown in meekness, or sown in wrath,
    In the broadest highway, or the shadowy path:
Refrain: Sure will the harvest be! (repeat three more times).

Emily S. Oakey

Day Is Dying In The West

In common with numerous popular people's hymns this
composition has been discarded by all modern denominational
hymn-book collections. Here, if you like, it makes a return,
and its inclusion should please many who have from all
accounts been searching for it. It seems best sung at the end
of a day of perfect weather when heaven and earth 'do' seem
to meet in a mysterious union.

Sennen   *W.F. Sherwin*

Day is dy-ing in the west, Heav'n is touch-ing earth with rest, Wait and wor-ship
while the night Sets her eve-ning lamps a-light Through all the sky.
Ho-ly, ho-ly, ho-ly, Lord God of hosts; Heav'n and earth are
full of Thee, Heav'n and earth are prais-ing Thee, O Lord most High.

2. Lord of life, beneath the dome
   Of the universe thy home,
   Gather us, who seek thy face,
   To the fold of thy embrace;
       For thou art nigh.
   Refrain

3. While the deepening shadows fall,
   Heart of love enfolding all,
   Through the glory and the grace
   Of the stars that veil thy face,
       Our hearts ascend.
   Refrain

4. When for ever from our sight
   Pass the stars, the day, the night,
   Lord of angels, on our eyes
   Let eternal morn arise,
       And shadows end.

                    W.F. Sherwin

Father Of Night

Christian convert and rock singer Bob Dylan wrote this
exquisite song while he was still involved with the Jewish faith.
No better analysis of the song exists than Anthony Scaduto's
comments in his book *Bob Dylan:* 'Bob Dylan in touch with
the Father, with the unknown which doesn't have to remain
unknown. A hymn of discovery, a hymn to the mysteries.'
This is the God of Abraham, Isaac and Jacob. Also Jesus.

Words and Music by
Bob Dylan

up in the sky,   Fa-ther of lone-li - ness___ and pain,   Fa-ther of love and

up in the sky,   Fa-ther of time,___   Fa-ther of dreams,   Fa-ther, who turn-eth the

CODA

1 Fa-ther of rain.

2 D.S. al Coda riv - ers and streams.

dwells in our hearts and our mem-o - ries,___

Fa-ther of min-utes,   Fa-ther of days,   Fa-ther of whom we most

sol-emn-ly praise.

143

Hear Us O Lord From Heaven

'That it may please Thee to give and preserve to our use
the kindly fruits of the earth, and to restore and continue
to use the blessings of the sea, so as in due time we may enjoy
them' – so reads a petition in the Litany of the Manx Church
(Isle of Man) and doubtless it was in the writer's mind, as it was
the old custom of Manx fisherman to ask God's blessing before
they cast their nets. By tradition verse three is usually sung by
men, but perhaps this practice in current society is not pleasing
to those furthering the feminist cause.

Peel Castle

Adapted by W.H. Gill, 1839-1923

Hear us, O Lord, from heav'n, Thy dwelling place: Like them of old, in
vain we toil all night, Unless with us Thou go, who art the
Light; Come then, O Lord, that we may see Thy face.

Eternal Father, Strong To Save

Not surprisingly this has become the 'hymn' of fishermen and those who set out to sea. It was sung in moving fashion at the memorial service for those who lost their lives in the Penlee life-boat disaster of December, 1981 when the entire crew died trying to rescue men and women from a shipwreck off the coast of south west Cornwall in Britain. Author William Whiting wrote this hymn for the 1861 edition of *Hymns Ancient And Modern.* He was Master of Winchester College Choristers' School.

Melita

J.B. Dykes, 1823-76

2. O Saviour, whose almighty word
The winds and waves submissive heard,
Who walkedst on the foaming deep,
And calm amid its rage didst sleep:
  O hear us when we cry to Thee
  For those in peril on the sea!

3. O Sacred Spirit, who didst brood
Upon the chaos dark and rude,
Who bad'st its angry tumult cease,
And gavest light, and life, and peace:
  O hear us when we cry to Thee
  For those in peril on the sea!

4. O Trinity of love and power,
Our brethren shield in danger's hour;
From rock and tempest, fire and foe,
Protect them wheresoe'er they go;
  And ever let there rise to Thee
  Glad hymns of praise from land and sea.

William Whiting, 1825-78

Jesus Saviour, Pilot Me

Dr. Eric Routley notes well the quality that distinguishes the
character of Jesus – he terms it 'this faculty of being at peace
with God, being obedient to God's routine, being at peace with
men and things, reverently and wonderingly, but never
capriciously or impatiently. That is the nature of the person who
is never shaken by the winds, who is never shocked by calamity,
who is never defeated by the demons.' In this context it can be
asked, 'Jesus, Saviour, Pilot Me'.

Jesus, Saviour, Pilot Me   J.E. Gould, 1822-75

Jes - us, Sav - iour, pi - lot me, O - ver life's tem - pes-tuous sea; Un - known

waves be - fore me roll,___ Hi - ding rock and treach-erous shoal;___ Chart and

com - pass come__from Thee: Jes - us, Sav - iour, pi - lot me!

2. As a mother stills her child,
   Thou canst hush the ocean wild;
   Boisterous waves obey thy will
   When thou sayest to them "Be still!"
   Wondrous Sovereign of the sea,
   Jesus, Saviour, pilot me.

3. When at last I near the shore,
   And the fearful breakers roar
   'Twixt me and the peaceful rest,
   Then, while leaning on thy breast,
   May I hear thee say to me,
   "Fear not, I will pilot thee."
                    Amen.

Edward Hopper, 1871

Will Your Anchor Hold

Baltimore teacher Priscilla Jane Owens wrote a number of fiery
emotive hymns including *We Have Heard A Joyful Sound*. For
fifty years she was actively involved in Sunday School work.

Will Your Anchor Hold

W.J. Kirkpatrick, 1838-1921

Will your an-chor hold in the storms of life, When the clouds un-fold their wings of strife? When the

strong tides lift, and the ca-bles strain, Will your an-chor drift or firm re-main?

REFRAIN

We have an an-chor that keeps the soul Stead-fast and sure while the bil-lows roll;

Fas-tened to the Rock which can-not move, Ground-ed firm and deep in the Sav-iour's love!

2. Will your anchor hold in the straits of fear?
   When the breakers roar and the reef is near;
   While the surges rave, and the wild winds blow,
   Shall the angry waves then your bark o'erflow?

3. Will your anchor hold in the floods of death,
   When the waters cold chill your latest breath?
   On the rising tide you can never fail,
   While your anchor holds within the veil.

4. Will your eyes behold through the morning light
   The city of gold and the harbour bright?
   Will you anchor safe by the heavenly shore,
   When life's storms are past for evermore?

Priscilla Jane Owens, 1829-99

Throw Out The Life Line!

People need the Gospel. People must be saved from their sins.
So – in part – said the 19th century revivalist preachers and
hymn-writers. Utilising imagery which means much to sea-faring
folk the writer urges Christians into the battle of saving souls.
Not a minute should be lost.

E.S. Ufford

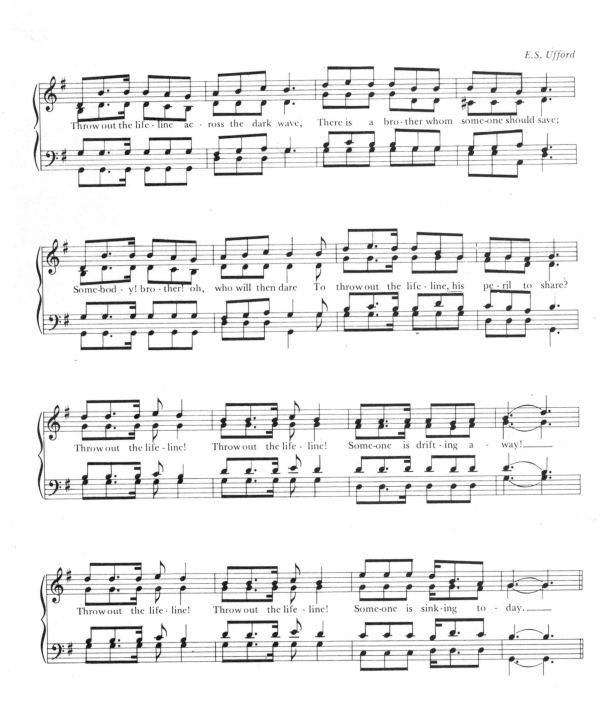

2. Throw out the life-line across the dark wave
   Why do you tarry, my brother so long?
   See he is sinking; oh hasten today —
   And out with the lifeboat! away then, away!

3. Throw out the life-line to danger-fraught men,
   Sinking in anguish where you've never been:
   Winds of temptation and billows of woe
   Will soon hurl them out where the dark waters flow.

4. Soon will the season of rescue be o'er,
   Soon will they drift to eternity's shore,
   Haste, then, my brother! no time for delay,
   But throw out the life-line, and save them today.

Rev. E.S. Ufford

Brightly Beams Our Father's Mercy

John Telford in *The New Methodist Hymn-Book Illustrated* (1934) says these verses were suggested to Philipp Bliss by an incident which he heard the preacher Daniel L. Moody tell: 'On a dark, stormy night, when the waves rolled like mountains and not a star was to be seen, a boat, rocking and plunging, neared the Cleveland harbour. "Are you sure this is Cleveland?" asked the captain, seeing only one light from the lighthouse. "Quite sure, sir," replied the pilot. "Can you make the harbour?" "We must, or perish, sir." The old pilot missed the channel and the boat crashed on the rocks and many a life was lost. "Brethren," said Mr. Moody, "the Master will take care of the great lighthouse; let the lower lights be burning." '

Let the Lower Lights   P. Bliss, 1838-76

Bright-ly beams our Fath-er's mer-cy From His light-house ev-er-more,___ But to us He gives the keep-ing of the lights a-long the shore. Let the low-er lights be burn-ing, Send a gleam ac-ross the wave; Some poor faint-ing, strugg-ling sea-man You may res-cue, you may save.

2. Dark the night of sin has settled,
    Loud the angry billows roar;
   Eager eyes are watching, longing,
    For the lights along the shore.

3. Trim your feeble lamp, my brother,
    Some poor sailor tempest tossed,
   Trying now to make the harbour,
    In the darkness may be lost.

Philipp Bliss, 1838-76

The gloom of the world
is but a shadow.
Behind it, yet within reach, is joy.
There is radiance
and glory in the darkness,
could we but see,
and to see, we have only to look
I beseech you
to look.

Fra Giovanni. 16th century

There is a tide
in the affairs of men,
Which, taken at the flood,
leads on to fortune;
Omitted,
all the voyage of their life
Is bound in shallows
and in miseries.
On such a full sea
are we now afloat;
And we must take the current
when it serves,
Or lose our ventures.

William Shakespeare
Julius Caesar, IV, iii

Away with my fears!
The glad morning appears,
When an heir of salvation was born!
From Jehovah I came,
For His glory I am,
And to Him I with singing return.

Charles Wesley

Glory to his name belongs,
Great, and marvellous, and high;
Sing unto the Lord your songs,
Cry, to every nation cry.
O the grace unsearchable!
While eternal ages roll,
God delights in man to dwell,
Soul of each believing soul.

Charles Wesley

God so loved the world that He gave us His only begotten
son that whosoever believeth in him should not perish
but have everlasting life.

St. John. 3 v:16

Teach us to know the Father, Son,
And thee, of both, to be but One;
That through the ages all along,
This, this may be our endless song:
    All praise to Thy eternal merit,
    O Father, Son, and Holy Spirit.

Anonymous, 9th or 10th century;
tr: John Cosin

Acknowledgments

The publishers would like to thank the following copyright holders for permission to use their work. The following hymns and songs must not be reprinted from this or any other source without due permission from the appropriate copyright holder:

Ding Dong Merrily On High (page 10), words by G.R. Woodward are reproduced by permission of SPCK.
Gaudete (pages 14-17), words and music Steeleye Span Music Ltd./Chrysalis Music Ltd.
Every Star Shall Sing A Carol (pages 18, 19), words and music by permission of Stainer & Bell Ltd.
Deck The Halls (pages 22, 23), music by kind permission of the Oxford University Press.
The Virgin Mary Had A Baby Boy (pages 36, 37), by kind permission. Words and music Boosey & Hawkes. From the Edric Connor Collection of West Indian Spirituals & Folk Tunes. Copyright 1945 Boosey & Company Ltd.
Now The Holly Bears A Berry (pages 38, 39), music by kind permission of the Oxford University Press.
Down In Yon Forest (page 40), music by permission of Stainer & Bell Ltd.
The Holly And The Ivy (pages 42, 43), by permission of Oxford University Press Music.
Joseph Dearest, Joseph Mine (pages 44, 45, 46), words and music, Oxford University Press.
I Saw Three Ships (page 49), music, Oxford University Press.

Unto Us A Boy Is Born (page 52), words and music by kind permission of the Oxford University Press.
Mary's Child (page 60), words and music Stainer & Bell Ltd.
See Amid The Winter's Snow (pages 72, 73), by kind permission words and music, M.A. Perry.
The Coventry Carol (page 80), words and tune by permission of Mowbrays Publishing.
He Is·Born (pages 82, 83), words by permission of the Oxford University Press.
Jesus, Jesus, Rest Your Head (pages 94, 95) music by kind permission of Banks Music Publications.
Cheer Up Friends (page 98), words and music by kind permission of the Oxford University Press.
Love Is Come Again (pages 104, 105), words and music by permission of the Oxford University Press.
A Toi La Gloire (pages 118, 119), words by permission of the Oxford University Press.
Father Of Night (pages 142, 143), by kind permission of Rams Horn, Big Sky Music, Words and Music.

All copyrights under Stainer & Bell Ltd. exclude USA. Copyright for the USA is given by Galaxy Music Corporation, 131 West 86th Street, New York, NY 10024, USA.

For any omission sincerest apologies are offered.

The publishers would like to thank the following individuals and organisations for their kind permission to reproduce the illustrations in this book on the following pages:

The Atkinson Art Gallery, Southport: 145, *The Fish Fag* by W.B. Fortesque.

BBC Hulton Picture Library: 11, *The Christmas Waits* by Henry Laurent; 63, *A Dream of Toys* from *The Graphic*, 25th December, 1869; 133, *Preparing for the Harvest Thanksgiving*.

The City Museums and Art Gallery, Birmingham: 147, *Disaster*. W. Langley.

Cooper-Bridgeman: 19, *The Waits* by S. Pearse; 39, *Girl with Holly in the Snow* by Ethel Parkinson; 65, Detail from *The Virgin and Child with Angels and Donors*. The Master of Castelsardo, 15th century. Birmingham City Art Gallery; 67, *Shepherd and his Flock in the Snow* by Vincent Haddelsey; 85, *Breton Village Under Snow*, 1894. Paul Gauguin. The Louvre, Paris; 105, *Spring Blossom* by Henri Richet; 115, *Easter Morning* by Caspar David Friedrich. By courtesy of Christies; 141, *Evening Near Barbazon* by Constant-Emile Troyon. From the collection of the Royal Holloway College, University of London; 157, *The Dance of Life* by Edward Munch. Nasjenalgalieriet, Oslo.

Mary Evans: 21, *Father Christmas Says Grace at the Christmas Dinner Tale* by E.F. Manning; 23, *The Font and the Flowers* by J. Leech; 25, *Preparing the Christmas Feast*, E.F. Manning; 31, *Jesus' Birth Announced to the Shepherds* by W.H. Boot; 69, *Snow Scene in Canada After Church* from *L'Illustration*, 1931; 79, *The Nativity* by M. Dibden Spooner; 87, illustration from *The Better Land*; 93, *The Three Wise Men* by Dulac.

Sonia Halliday Photographs: 27, *The Nativity* by Giotto. Fresco in the transept of the Lower Church at Assisi; 35, *Annunciation to the Shepherds* by Burne-Jones, All Hallows Church, Allerton, Liverpool; 53, *The Nativity*. A panel in the east window of St. Peter Mancroft, Norwich; 61, Castle Howard, York. *The Nativity* by Burne-Jones, 1874; 111, *Carrying the Cross*, Lorenzetti School, 14th century Assisi; 117, Detail of *The Sergeant in the Battle of Britain Window* by Hugh Easton. Westminster Abbey; 121, *The Resurrection*, Kloster Kirche Konigsfelden, Switzerland.

Mansell Collection: 2, *Star in the East*. Cathedrale Sommeil des Mages, Autun. France; 9, *The Adoration of the Magi;* 13,

The Waits by H.G. Hine; 17, *The Magi*, a woodcut; 43, *Preparing for Christmas;* 47, *The Shepherds by the Crib;* 51, *The Appearance of the Angel to the Shepherds*, after P. Lagarde; 77, *The Million*, a Christmas carol, 1893; 81, *Adoration of the Magi;* 91, *Three Kings Mosaic*. Ravenna; 107, *Illustration to the Manger;* 125, *Illustration to the Gleaners;* 131, *Harvest Decorations at St. Michael's Church*, illustration.

National Gallery, London: 99, *Master of Liesborn;* 119, painting by Bruyn.

The Newlyn Orion Gallery, Penzance; 155, *A Fish Sale on a Cornish Beach*. Stanhope Forbes.

Penzance Town Council; 151, *Tuck in Pilchards* by Percy Craft.

Peter Newark's Historical Pictures; 83, *The Virgin and Child*. 13th century.

Private Collection: 149, *The Call of the Sea* by Frederick Cayley Robinson.

The Royal Academy, London: 73, *When Snow the Pasture Sheets* by Joseph Farquarson.

The Tate Gallery, London: 109, *The Crucifixion* by Stanley Spencer; 153, *A Ship Aground* by J.M.W. Turner.

Scala: 37, *The Adoration of the Shepherds* by Lotto; 41, *The Month of January* by Trento; 55, *Adoration of the Shepherds*, Perugia by Fiorenzo di Lorenzo; 57, *The Magi* by P. Brueghel; 75, *The Arrival at Bethlehem* by P. Brueghel; 137, *La Mietitura* by Luglio; 139, *The Harvest Moon* by John Linnel. The Victoria and Albert Museum, London.

The following artists were specifically commissioned to supply the illustrations on the pages listed below:

Rosalind Bliss, 127
Moira Chesmur, 33
Ros Forster, 97
Jerry Hoare, 48, 122
Charlotte Styles, 103

The editor and publishers have taken every care to locate and acknowledge the sources for the material used in this book. If, however, an incorrect attribution has been made we will gladly rectify the mistake in future reprints, provided that we receive notification.